THE AGE OF INNOCENCE

A Novel of Ironic Nostalgia

TWAYNE'S MASTERWORK STUDIES

Robert Lecker, General Editor

THE AGE OF INNOCENCE

A Novel of Ironic Nostalgia

Linda Wagner-Martin

TWAYNE PUBLISHERS
An Imprint of Simon & Schuster Macmillan
New York

PRENTICE HALL INTERNATIONAL
London Mexico City New Delhi Singapore Sydney Toronto

Twayne's Masterwork Studies No. 162

The Age of Innocence: A Novel of Ironic Nostalgia
Linda Wagner-Martin

Copyright © 1996 by Linda Wagner-Martin

Twayne Publishers
An Imprint of Simon & Schuster Macmillan
1633 Broadway
New York, New York 10019

Library of Congress Cataloging-in-Publication Data
Wagner-Martin, Linda.
     The age of innocence : a novel of ironic nostalgia / Linda Wagner
-Martin.
     p. cm.— (Masterworks studies ; no. 162)
     Includes bibliographical references (p.) and index.
     ISBN 0-8057-4616-1 (cloth). — ISBN 0-8057-4615-3 (paper)
     1. Wharton, Edith, 1862–1937. Age of innocence. 2. Nostalgia in
literature. 3. Irony in literature. I. Title. II. Series:
     Twayne's masterwork studies ; no. 162.
PS3545.H16A738 1996
813'.52—dc20   95-46868
                                                      CIP

The paper used in this publication meets the minimum requirements of American National Standard for Information Sciences—Permanence of Paper for Printed Library Materials. ANSI. Z3948–1984. ∞ ™

10 9 8 7 6 5 4 3 2 1 (hc)
10 9 8 7 6 5 4 3 2 1 (pb)

Printed in the United States of America

For Karla and Janet

Contents

Acknowledgments

I am indebted throughout this study to the work of Shari Benstock, Margaret McDowell, and Cynthia Griffin Wolff. Many thanks to the Lilly Library, Indiana University, for permission to reproduce the photograph of Edith Wharton, and to the Harry Ransom Humanities Research Center, University of Texas, Austin, for permission to quote from Wharton's letters.

Note on the References

References to *The Age of Innocence* throughout this text are from the Collier Books (Macmillan) paperback edition, 1993, based on the sixth printing of the first edition (D. Appleton and Co.), which incorporates the author's revisions.

Edith Wharton

Chronology: Edith Wharton's Life and Works

1862 Edith Newbold Jones, born January 24, at 14 West 23rd Street, New York City, third and last child of Lucretia Stevens Rhinelander and George Jones.

1866–72 Travels in Europe (Italy, Spain, France, Germany) with her family as a result of the post–Civil War depression, which had a severe impact on her father's real estate investments. Her childhood passion for "making up" and reciting narratives and poems begins long before she can read; her father teaches her to read.

1872–79 After returning to the United States, the family spends winters in New York and summers in Newport. Edith writes her 30,000-word novella *Fast and Loose* in 1876–77.

1879 With her mother as publisher, Edith collects her poems as *Verses*. She makes her social debut.

1880–82 Faced with George Jones' failing health, the family lives abroad until his death in spring of 1882. In August, Edith's engagement to Harry Stevens is announced, despite his mother's objections; in October, the engagement is broken.

1883 Edith meets Walter Berry at Bar Harbor, but he does not propose. Later in the season, she meets Teddy Wharton.

1885 Edith and Teddy are married on April 29 and begin their life as a socially prominent couple.

1886–88 Edith lives at Pencraig, in New York City, and at Land's End, a Newport estate, and spends time in Europe each year. She inherits $120,000 from a cousin; this, added to her $20,000 from her father, enables the Whartons to take a four-month Aegean cruise.

1889–92	Renting a small house in New York City, Edith publishes poems and short stories and completes a novella, "Bunner Sisters," but she suffers from nausea and ennui.
1893	Buys Land's End and, with Ogden Codman's help, redecorates it.
1894–96	Wharton continues writing stories, which Edward Burlingame suggests she collect and allow Scribner's to publish. Her intermittent nausea, melancholia, and exhaustion slows her creative progress.
1897	With Codman, Edith writes *The Decoration of Houses*, which Scribner's publishes. Resumes friendship with Walter Berry.
1898	Plans collected stories, *The Greater Inclination*. As an outpatient, Edith is treated for a breakdown by S. Weir Mitchell.
1899	*The Greater Inclination* is published. Lives in Washington, D.C., for a time.
1900	*The Touchstone* is published. Wharton's illness continues.
1901	Wharton builds The Mount, a source of pride and pleasure for many years, in Lenox, Massachusetts. *Crucial Instances* (stories) is published; her mother dies in Paris.
1902	*Valley of Decision* is published; Henry James praises it but advises her to "Do New York," to use what she knows as subject. Her illness continues, though she begins a novel about modern life in New York (*Disintegration*), which is never finished. Her translation of Sudermann's play, *Es Lebe das Leben*, is produced on Broadway and published. Teddy has the first of his breakdowns.
1903–4	Travels in Italy and meets Bernard Berenson. *Sanctuary*, *The Descent of Man* (stories), and *Italian Villas and Their Gardens* are published. Buys an automobile and sells Land's End.
1905	*The House of Mirth* is a huge commercial success. Spends time abroad; develops a friendship with Henry James, who visits at The Mount.
1906	*Madame de Treymes* is published. Edith's illness continues.
1907	*The Fruit of the Tree* is published. Edith, Teddy, and Henry James tour southern France; frequent visits between James and Wharton. Meets Morton Fullerton, a younger journalist.
1908–10	Short-lived affair with Fullerton. Teddy is plagued by depression, breakdowns; he confesses to embezzling her funds and having affairs. *Artemis to Acteon* (poems) and *The Hermit and the Wild Woman* (stories) are published. Moves to 53 rue de Varenne in Faubourg Saint-Germain, Paris, where she lives until 1920.

Chronology

1911	After a separation, Edith and Teddy reconcile. *Ethan Frome* is published.
1912	The Mount is sold; *The Reef* is published. Edith and Teddy separate.
1913	Edith and Teddy are divorced on April 16, on grounds of Teddy's adultery. *The Custom of the Country* is published, and she begins *Literature*, which she never finishes. Travels with Berry, Berenson; returns to New York for family wedding.
1914	Travels to Algiers with Percy Lubbock and Gaillard Lapsley, and to Majorca with Berry. Organizes war relief in Paris during World War I.
1915	*Fighting France* is published; continues war relief efforts.
1916	*The Book of the Homeless* is published; Wharton finds places for 750 Belgian orphans. Henry James dies in England.
1917	Wharton is awarded the Order of Leopold, Belgium, and the French Legion of Honor. *Summer* and *Xingo and Other Stories* are published.
1918	Buys Pavillon Colombe near Paris; publishes *The Marne*.
1919	*French Ways and Their Meaning* is published.
1920	Wharton restores medieval monastery at Hyeris on the Riviera for a summer home. Publishes *The Age of Innocence* and *In Morocco*.
1921	Awarded Pulitzer Prize for Fiction for *The Age of Innocence*. "The Old Maid" is published.
1922	*The Glimpses of the Moon* is published.
1923	Film version of *Glimpses*, with subtitles by F. Scott Fitzgerald. Returns to United States (her last visit) to accept an honorary doctorate from Yale University. Publishes *A Son at the Front*.
1924	*Old New York* (four novellas) is published. Receives Gold Medal from National Institute of Arts and Letters.
1925	Publishes *The Mother's Recompense* and *The Writing of Fiction*.
1926	Elected to the National Institute of Arts and Letters. Publishes *Here and Beyond* and *Twelve Poems*. Takes a yacht trip on the Aegean.
1927	Walter Berry dies. *Twilight Sleep* is published.
1928	Teddy Wharton dies. *The Children* is published.
1929	Though seriously ill, Wharton continues writing. *Hudson River Bracketed* is published.

1930   Elected to the American Academy of Arts and Letters. *Certain People* is published.

1932   *The Gods Arrive* is published.

1933   *Human Nature* is published.

1934   *Backward Glance*, Wharton's autobiography, is published.

1936   *The World Over* is published.

1937   *Ghosts* and *The Buccaneers* are published. Wharton dies on August 11, following a stroke, and is buried at Versailles next to the ashes of Walter Berry. Her papers are left to Yale University, with all publication rights withheld until 1968.

LITERARY AND HISTORICAL CONTEXT

1

Historical Context

1920 was an apt time for nostalgia. When Edith Wharton began writing her novel about 1870s New York, which she would eventually call—somewhat ironically—*The Age of Innocence*, most of the world still reeled from the devastation of The Great War. The conflict that had killed 10 million soldiers and civilians and wounded 20 million others, by conservative estimates, had surprised the complacent, civilized culture in which Wharton moved; no one had believed war on this scale was possible. Living in France, Wharton experienced the destruction, fear, and resulting human loss of all kinds more vividly than she would have by just reading about the conflict from some safe American location; and true to her nature, she was moved from the start of hostilities in 1914 to do something about the waste of lives and opportunities she saw around her.

By 1914, Wharton was a successful, acclaimed novelist whose income from her writing allowed her to live in luxury. As a writer, she was a skilled observer of people and customs; in wartime Europe, however, Wharton did much more than observe. With her characteristic energy (and no small amount of organizing ability), she established the large supervisory American Hostels for Refugees program. During

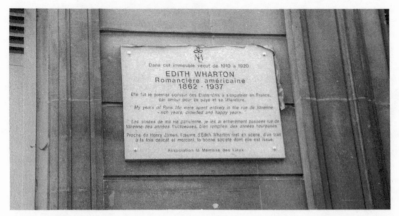

Plaque at Wharton's Paris address installed in 1991 by the Wharton Society.

Courtesy of Linda Wagner-Martin.

its first year, she raised $100,000 to fund its helpful programs, which included providing care facilities for tubercular soldiers and civilians; workrooms for unemployed women; actual gifts of housing, food, clothing, medical and child care; and employment opportunities for more than 10,000 refugees.

Because the German forces had first invaded the neutral country of Belgium, Wharton saw the great need in that area and in 1915 helped found the Children of Flanders Rescue Committee. That year it established six homes that provided shelter and training for 750 Flemish children, most of them orphans.[1] As Wharton the writer understood so well, many of the casualties of war were not among the dead. It was the terror of the living deaths surrounding her that she wanted to ameliorate.

She continued to initiate such programs, true rescue efforts, until she was exhausted—mentally, physically, emotionally, and financially. Wharton had been working hard on two fronts: Wharton had combined her practical relief efforts with her writing. Either she was working to set up a new home for the Belgian orphans, or she was writing essays about conditions in France or editing *The Book of the Homeless,* which contained contributions from many European writers (the proceeds from this 1916 publication went directly to war relief).

By the end of the war in 1919, Wharton was in her late 50s, and she was in an introspective mood. This mood stemmed partly from her own weariness but mostly from her immersion in the crucible of war. When she decided to write the book that became *The Age of Innocence,* she was trying to find relief from the massive sorrow that had, necessarily, enveloped her. (Although she had planned to write a novel about a war-torn family, it was several years before she began *A Son at the Front,* a book focusing on a mother's fears for her son rather than on his battlefield experiences. As in her non-fiction prose, here, too, she emphasizes the emotional costs of war.)

Writing about New York in the 1870s gave Wharton a chance to return to a more imaginative work, and to place herself in a time when, and a country where, people saw life as promising. New York in the 1870s was already famous as the enclave of the moneyed elite "400." Edith Newbold Jones (born in 1862) had been a member of this society because her mother was a Rhinelander and her father, a Jones. Summering in Newport and spending winters abroad or in their lower-Eighties address in New York City, the Joneses tried to live as sumptuously as their neighbors and friends. (They lived so elegantly, in fact, that the phrase "keeping up with the Joneses" grew out of their influence on many New Yorkers, some of whom were richer than they.)

For Wharton to go back in time to the days of her lavish, and lavishly protected, childhood was itself a luxury. The New York she describes so carefully in *The Age of Innocence* is truly "prewar." War of the magnitude the world had just survived in 1919 was unimaginable to the successful people of 1870s New York. Their affluence seemed to suggest that some higher power was rewarding their behavior: financial prosperity became an index of moral probity. Yet seen even in the most positive light, those distant New York years were also filled with cruelty, duplicity, and self-aggrandizement. Morality was often only a veneer. Wharton saw as she studied the culture of the

1870s that, in some ways, the age of apparent innocence and propriety had foreshadowed the brutality of the coming war.

The truth of Wharton's vision was that blood sacrifice played a big role in the power structure of New York's "400." The primary social value was the appearance of respectability. Whether or not one was truly respectable or moral was seldom the issue. This was a society governed by rules that were rarely questioned, rules made by the same elite that benefited from them. Wharton learned as she wrote her novel that there was little charitable or humane about New York's high society during the 1870s.

Another part of Wharton's process of remembering was her increasingly negative reaction to life in the United States. When she returned in 1913 for her niece's wedding, having lived much of each year since 1906 in France, she found New York "queer, rootless" and, in some respects, "overwhelming."[2] More comfortable with the highly cultured luxury of the expatriate Americans living in both London and Paris, Wharton wondered why she had ever thought herself "at home" in the United States. Her personal discontent colored her retrospective view of 19th-century New York, in which she claimed to have found the roots of the present culture.

2

The Importance of *The Age of Innocence*

Wharton's novel has been a focus of American readers' interest since it won the Pulitzer Prize for Fiction in 1921. Even though Wharton was already considered a notable writer, the award brought the book greater scholarly and academic attention.

The prize called attention to *The Age of Innocence* in another way: the jury had originally planned to give it to Sinclair Lewis's shockingly modernist *Main Street,* a novel that questions the traditional values of a small Midwestern town. When some jurors protested that Lewis's work was troubling, the prize went to Wharton's novel because it could be considered "uplifting" to American morals. Wharton wrote to Lewis that she was in despair about the circumstances—and about her fiction's being thought "uplifting."[1] The friendship that grew between the established writer and Lewis was based on respect for each other's work; later that year Lewis dedicated his novel *Babbitt* to Wharton.[2] She thanked him graciously but warned him that the American public found irony "as unintelligible as Chinese."[3]

At this stage in her career, Edith Wharton wanted to be taken seriously. She longed for consideration by established critics; she wanted to win the accolades that—after the Pulitzer—began to come to her. In 1923 she returned to the United States to become the first woman to receive an honorary doctorate of letters from Yale University. In 1924 she received the Gold Medal for Fiction from the National Institute of Arts and Letters, and in 1926 she was elected to that group. In 1930 she was elected to the American Academy of Arts and Letters. Most of these honors spoke about *The Age of Innocence*; the novel became a linchpin in her reputation, a central work in her oeuvre. In fact, after its publication in 1920, many of her critics later spoke of Wharton's "decline" as a novelist, implying that the fiction that followed this masterpiece was inferior to it.[4]

Part of the appeal of the work was its focus on a part—an admittedly prosperous part—of American history. The image of Wharton as a committed and accurate chronicler of American life helped erase the sometimes suspicious reading of Wharton as a wealthy woman who continued to make a great deal of money by writing fiction that could be read "popularly." Although many did read it, *The Age of Innocence* is so based in an historical past that its appeal could be considered historical. It also reifies the values of that past. Although Wharton seems to support the values of May Welland and her family, if one looks closely at the text one can see that she simultaneously questions them. Thanks to the subtlety of her narrative, readers of all kinds could find what they wanted in her fiction, and what they wanted to find in *The Age of Innocence* was that veritable "age," a time more orderly and moral than the incipient Roaring Twenties that were soon to shock them.

This novel also showed Wharton to good advantage, as different from the young modernist writers such as Sinclair Lewis, whose chief aim seemed to be scathing criticism of American life both present and past. Wharton lived abroad, but she seldom identified with the outspoken young American expatriates who made complaints about their country the mainstay of their writing. She was a writer people could use to reclaim and revise the American past in a positive way.

And Wharton was due some attention. Many of the younger modernists had long admired her work, as they had that of Henry James. Not that she was in any sense a replica of James, but the two writers' concern with characters' psychological complexities was the foundation of much 20th-century writing. If young writers wanted to be instructed in the modernist method, they read T. S. Eliot, James Joyce, Henry James, Edith Wharton, and Willa Cather—but only a few of them admitted to the latter two influences.[5]

Not only did *The Age of Innocence* win the Pulitzer, it was also serialized (for the huge sum of $18,000) in *Pictorial Review*. Appleton, her publisher, also paid Wharton a $15,000 advance, and the book quickly sold more than 100,000 copies in the United States and England. Two years after its publication, the book had earned $50,000, a sum that included the $9,000 which Warner Brothers film studio paid for the movie rights.[6] Wharton's 1920 novel was hardly a sleeper; people had read it, or had seen the film version, throughout the modernist decades. By the time it was taught in classrooms, it already had a long popular history.

Most important, *The Age of Innocence* was, and is, a thoroughly interesting novel. Regardless of Wharton's fame at this point in her career, or the inherent glamour of the late 19th-century culture that is the book's focus, this novel succeeds because it captures the reader's imagination. The reader cares what becomes of Newland Archer and Ellen Olenska; convinced that their love for each other is genuine, the reader hangs on each turn of the plot, each twist of Wharton's irony, hoping beyond all reasonable expectation that the characters will find a way to be together. In *The Age of Innocence*, Wharton has created a compelling love story whose appeal seems timeless. It is significant as a portrait of a culture and a period; it is more remarkable, however, for the sheer romance of its complicated—and therefore realistic—story.

3

Critical Reception

Critics' reactions to *The Age of Innocence* can serve as a kind of Rorschach inkblot test to changing taste during the 20th century. In the 1920s, a period much like the 1870s in its valorization of financial success and tendency to legislate morals, readers justified Newland Archer and May Welland staying together. Rather than seeing any irony in Archer's living by the values that he questions at the beginning of the novel, they accepted his wife's earnest, moral thinking. Many readers overlooked May's outright lie to Ellen Olenska about her pregnancy, excusing her subterfuge because she is saving her marriage. Ellen, moreover, was thought to be an unsympathetic character, regardless of Wharton's apparent preference for her.[1]

Later, in the 1940s, when one could once again read literature for pleasure after the debacles of both the 1930s depression and World War II, *The Age of Innocence* was called a masterpiece. A mellowing fondness for "Americans"—even those with negative characteristics—made readers appreciate fiction about truly American personae and themes.

Temporarily eclipsed during the 1950s by the critical excitement over such modernists as F. Scott Fitzgerald, Ernest Hemingway, and

William Faulkner (writers whose books became the core of classes in a new field of study, American literature), Wharton's writing resurfaced in the latter decades of the 20th century. Then, feminism rivaled modernism for scholars' attention; in some ways, *The Age of Innocence* satisfied both interests. Not only was it written by a woman, with two strong women characters facing moral dilemmas involving sexual choices; but its style approaches the precise, elliptical, and highly polished modernist narrative.[2]

But when *The Age of Innocence* first appeared in 1920, critics were less sympathetic to the women characters. Although the novel was praised, attention was paid mostly to the dilemma facing Newland Archer. He is the center of consciousness, if not the hero; and his narrative movement from naïve yet worldly bachelor to husband trapped in a conventional, dulling marriage was seen as the true plot of the text. Reviewers said less about character, in fact, than they did about Wharton's place in literary history. Henry Seidel Canby compared her with Jane Austen; William Lyon Phelps, with Joseph Conrad and Henry James.[3]

Critics were also fascinated with her complex view of elite society. *The Times Literary Supplement* called the novel "a thorough mastery of the whole situation"; the *Spectator* admired her portrayal of tribal loyalties and social battles.[4] A. E. W. Mason, writing in *Bookman,* praised Wharton's re-creation of the era, although he found the story itself less accomplished.[5] *The New Republic*'s reviewer (F. H.), in contrast, deemed this study of the "best people" to be "a superb subject" for "Mrs. Wharton."[6] For Canby, Wharton's scrutiny of the power of the American family reflected values of both class and religion. Although he could see that readers might consider her focus narrow, Canby pointed out that such a focus was never "small." Carl Van Doren, too, admired Wharton's world of "uncompromising decorum."[7]

The recognition of Wharton's mastery brought with it a natural qualification. Such a limited society is marked by what William Lyon Phelps termed "artificial and false standards," leading inevitably to a kind of stagnation for Wharton's characters.[8] Van Doren, in his first review of the book, said that the characters were "stiff with ceremonial garments and heavy with the weight of imagined responsibilities."[9] Katherine Mansfield had the same objection as she called for more passion ("a little wildness, a dark place or two in the soul").[10] As these critics suggested, drawing characters appropriate to a period piece gave the novelist an inherent handicap.

For many reviewers, *The Age of Innocence* was a triumph of form. This was Mason's term, and it was echoed by Canby, R. D. Townsend, and Frederick Watson, who made the point that Wharton's characters were so real the reader forgot the half a century of distance from them.[11]

For others, form was marred by what they saw as an implausible ending. Edwin Francis Edgett called the conclusion "lame and impotent," and the anonymous reviewer for the *Spectator* said directly that Archer surely would have visited Ellen, if only out of curiosity.[12] With this criticism, and in the midst of general praise for Wharton's skillful depiction of the 1870s, came a few mutterings about "historical inaccuracies."[13]

After a great many highly positive reviews, reservations began to set in. The biographical fallacy took hold: reviewers could not forget who Edith Wharton was—a part of the fashionable society that ruled New York, a society mere literary people could seldom join. In fact, Vernon Parrington titled his review "Our Literary Aristocrat" and found fault with the very subject of Wharton's novel, which he described as "its little clan of first families that gently simmers in its own dullness." For him, it was Wharton's "aloofness from her own America" that kept her from being a great writer. Rather than comprehending that she saw the travesties of the culture and worked hard to represent them, Parrington identified her only as a member of the elite group.[14]

The Age of Innocence collected reviews as it did sales, and moved Wharton from being thought of as a woman writer who produced somewhat remote psychological studies of relationships—as in *The Reef* (1912), *The Custom of the Country* (1913), and *Summer* (1916)—to one who drew entire segments of culture accurately. She became the serious cultural historian of her time, and, with the death of James in 1916, the best writer of traditional fiction in America.

Arthur Hobson Quinn, writing in one of the publicity pamphlets then popular in U.S. publishing, claimed that Wharton was "the foremost living novelist writing in the English language." He then asked "which of us are as truly alive as Lily Bart, as Ethan Frome, as Ellen Olenska, as May Welland? And which of us will live as long?"[15]

Although Quinn singled out the women characters of *The Age of Innocence* for praise, most reviewers foregrounded Wharton's treatment of society as a whole. Individuality was, then, folded into a kind of blurred impressionism—a tactic that was evidently useful to critics by allowing them to talk about these remote times and societies with an air of distance, even condescension. It was also a way to relegate Wharton, despite her proven narrative competence, to the same kind of historical past. That she felt such relegation seems clear from her comment to Sinclair Lewis:

> What you say is so kind, so generous & so unexpected, that I don't know where to begin to answer. It is the first sign I have ever had—literally—that "les jeunes" at home had ever read a word of me. I had long since resigned myself to the idea that I was regarded by you all as the—say the Mrs. Humphrey Ward of the Western Hemisphere; though at times I wondered why. . . .[16]

Clearly, Wharton, too, had been reading the reviewers.

This emphasis in the reviews of *The Age of Innocence* on Wharton's perceived fascination with the past may have led to her shift to themes that were clearly based on events in the present: *The Glimpses of the Moon, The Mother's Recompense, Twilight Sleep,* and *The Children* (novels published in 1922, 1925, 1927, and 1928) all deal with the modern problems caused by the ease with which divorces were granted, and the resulting fragmentation of family structures. They also reflect Wharton's wartime experiences with the pain of mothers separated from their children, mothers unable to care for their children, and the abandonment of the young—whether intentional or inadvertent. Partly because these themes were atypical of the Wharton novels reviewers had earlier defined, her books published later in the 1920s were seldom reviewed positively.

Once Wharton died in 1937, however, it was hard for readers to forget "Mrs. Wharton," as she was known throughout much of the 20th century. Critics as diverse as Edmund Wilson, Alfred Kazin, Blake Nevius, Q. D. Leavis, Lionel Trilling, Louis Auchincloss, and Diana Trilling were writing about her through the 1940s, 1950s, and 1960s. It was Wilson in his 1947 *The Wound and the Bow* who remarked on her consistent creation of the weak male character. Seeing the strong woman–ineffectual man as a pattern (in more works than just *The Age of Innocence*), Wilson concluded that "There are no first-rate men in these novels." Whether or not her lack of forceful males led him to his final opinion, he paid Wharton homage only to bury her, saying that her work would not last and that even *The Age of Innocence* "is already rather faded."[17]

In a seminal book-length study, Blake Nevius explored the novelist's achievements through a focus on her consummate use of irony.[18] Other critics contributed to a generally positive understanding of her accomplishments, but it was Arthur Mizener's inclusion of Wharton's 1920 novel in his *Twelve Great American Novels* (1967)—11 of these written by men—that codified critical opinion. Tracing her work from its beginning, Mizener allowed that her innate dignity and role as an upper-class woman may have limited her professional greatness, but there was no question about her "easy and richly conscious" narrative. In choosing *The Age of Innocence* as her best work, Mizener spoke of Wharton's "ability really to create these lives, rather than merely to assert that they exist." He commented, too, on the "beautifully realized . . . mature passion and moral realism"[19] of Ellen and Newland, drawing the reader into the poignance of both their passion and their renunciation.

Over the past 30 years, criticism of this masterpiece has been steady but diverse, its nuances reflecting the perspectives of several generations of critics.

A READING

4

Edith Wharton's View of *The Age of Innocence*

She had called an early version *Old New York*, and when she wrote to her good friend and sister-in-law Mary Cadwalader Jones ("Minnie") about the book, she described evocatively her memories of that childhood world. Writing the novel that became *The Age of Innocence* set Wharton's imagination to work at full speed, despite the fact that she could barely remember the years she was trying to capture. Born in 1862, Wharton had been a child during the early 1870s.

The vestiges of that all-but-lost world, such an important element in *The Age of Innocence*, are in some ways the kinds of details a child might remember: Newport's lush lawns heading to the huge, bright sea, lacquered tables accented with silver ornaments, an elegant white-waistcoated gentleman with a flower in his buttonhole. The child Edith, who early on yearned to be a writer, would have been sensitive to the gold-trimmed boxes in the old Academy of Music. She might have recalled the expectant hush as the curtain began its ascent, and she would surely have recalled key emotional scenes from the plays and operas she saw as a late adolescent. As she reminisces in "Life and I," "I always saw the visible world as a series of pictures, more or less harmoniously composed."[1]

Her scrutiny of New York was intensified by having lived abroad for much of her childhood. The Joneses survived some financial losses by traveling in Europe from Edith's fifth year through her 10th and renting out their expensive homes, one in New York and the other, a "cottage," in Newport. With exchange rates favoring U.S. currency, living a luxurious existence in Europe cost less than leading the life of the American upper class at home. As Wharton recalled, she was so susceptible to beauty as a child that when she returned to the United States (at 10) she could only think "How ugly it is!" Although she had been "keenly interested in the change" to American life, she then faced what she called "bitter disappointment" and came to think of herself as "an exile in America" (*LI*, 1080–81). What she minded most was the "mean monotonous streets, without architecture, without great churches or palaces, or any visible memorials of an historic past."[2]

The years of travel also trained the young Edith as an observer. From childhood, she was one on whom nothing was lost. In one of her memoirs, she describes herself as being driven by "certain images— impressions of scenery, and more sharply-drawn visions of rooms . . ." (*LI*, 1072). In fact, she describes her literal memory as "vague pictures of travel . . . my visual sensibility seems to me, as I look back, to have been as intense then as it is now" (*LI*, 1071).

The text of *The Age of Innocence* is in some ways a palimpsest of Wharton's memories—childhood glimpses and intuitions layered with the more aware, and often cynical, perspective of the emerging woman, the Edith Newbold Jones who found herself too long on the marriage market. (After her debut at 17—her mother moved that event up a year rather than have her spend her time writing—Wharton was unduly conscious of the ticking matrimonial clock.) Her compelling look back into the 1870s is in many ways as autobiographical as Ernest Hemingway's young Nick Adams, fishing and watching babies being born in the Michigan wilds. For upper-class women of the late 19th century, including Wharton, the test of personal worth was becoming engaged. The sometimes sly undercurrent of criticism that gives the novel its edge is a running commentary on the strategies the wealthy class employed to "protect" its young, marriageable women—

even in the midst of intense, and often illicit, sexual activity and financial chicanery.

Wharton portrays in vivid detail the blushing naïf, May Welland, holding her daily bouquet of lilies-of-the-valley as though her soul were as virginal as her imagination. Readers are introduced to May as "a young girl in white with eyes ecstatically fixed on the stagelovers . . . a warm pink mounted to the girl's cheek, mantled her brow to the roots of her fair braids, and suffused the young slope of her breast to the line where it met a modest tulle tucker fastened with a single gardenia. She dropped her eyes to the immense bouquet of lilies-of-the-valley on her knee, and Newland Archer saw her white-gloved fingertips touch the flowers softly." When she feels Newland's eyes upon her, she blushes more deeply. And then Wharton makes clear why May has been described in this overwrought, almost archaic prose—because this is the tenor of Newland's voice when he considers her, his fiancée, his beloved, his woman. The paragraph closes with this sentence: "He drew a breath of satisfied vanity and his eyes returned to the stage."[3]

Wharton's fictional game throughout the novel is to use Newland Archer as a center of consciousness but then undercut his impressions. His romance with May Welland exists to please his vanity; it has little to do with love. Wharton shows the reader early on that Newland, for his part, is the veteran of at least one affair with a married woman and the vicarious veteran of most of the famed love affairs in Western literature. Priding himself on his expertise in matters of the heart, Newland dreams of somehow sculpting the inexperienced May into some "miracle of fire and ice" (7) that will satisfy both his sexual and his intellectual urges, as well as his need to control her, his life, and his destiny.

The society of Newport and New York is filled with men who victimize their women. Although she downplays the truth of this generalization, in episode after episode Wharton returns to this theme. Readers often miss the cutting intent of her narrative, partly because she adopts an objective tone, and partly because she focuses so specifically on the details of the social scene that one's attention is absorbed by the what of the culture rather than the why or how. When the New

York men gossip about the possibility that Ellen Olenska lived with the male secretary who helped her escape from her husband, the reader remembers the men smoking good cigars "near the fire in the Gothic library" while the women (the subjects of their discourse) "trailed their long silk draperies up to the drawing-room," complete with "a Carcel lamp with an engraved globe" (41).

Similarly, at the van der Luydens' dinner for the duke (and the often-snubbed Countess Olenska), Wharton devotes much space to describing the "du Lac Sèvres and the Trevenne George II plate . . . the van der Luyden 'Lowestoft' (East India Company) and the Dagonet Crown Derby" (61). As Louis Auchincloss notes in *Edith Wharton; A Woman in Her Time,* her descriptions are as accurate as color slides, and she purposefully brings New York and Newport to life. But she contrasts their rich "color and detail that delights the imagination" with what he calls "the smallness and vapidity" of her characters. Auchincloss writes:

> Mr. Welland is a querulous hypochondriac, with no opinions but many habits, and his wife has to find her fulfillment in being his slave. Sillerton Jackson brings to the study of scandal the science of a naturalist. . . . Mr. van der Luyden, through his obsequious consort and intermediary, rules society with the naivete, simplicity, and pomposity of a true Victorian monarch. Even old Catherine Mingott, the ancestress and dowager, known to an awed New York as "Catherine the Great," is not, in the last analysis, so very formidable. Her bluster and independence are little more than poses, and in the big decisions she is swayed by her son and her lawyer.[4]

Despite the truth of Auchincloss's comment, *The Age of Innocence* manages to maintain the sense of its title. It is as if a comparatively innocent observer is scrutinizing these scenes, searching for the reason why one behavior is "proper" or one dress "suitable," others "inappropriate." The observer as child chooses the focus; as Wharton recalls in *A Backward Glance,* many of her impressions of the time came from those scenes furtively glimpsed as the child she then was, "peeped at from the stairtop while wraps were removed in the hall below . . . rosy and white-whiskered gentlemen . . . ladies with bare sloping shoulders rising flower-like from voluminous skirts" (*ABG*, 830). Her love of list-making in the novel, then, is both a tribute to her power of recollection and a wry apology for a society that accorded great value to such trivia. In the scene where Newland checks off his wedding preparations, this acerbity comes through clearly:

> The bridesmaids' eight bouquets of white lilac and lilies-of-the-valley had been sent in due time, as well as the gold and sapphire sleeve-links of the eight ushers and the best man's cat's-eye scarf-pin; Archer had sat up half the night trying to vary the wording of his thanks for the last batch of presents from men friends and ex-lady-loves; the fees for the Bishop and the Rector were safely in the pocket of his best man; his own luggage was already at Mrs. Manson Mingott's, where the wedding breakfast was to take place. . . . (179–80)

Although Wharton trusted her memory, she also had the willing help of her best friend, Minnie, in research that could be done only in the United States. Living in France, Wharton was cut off from information that might confirm or supplement her own knowledge. Minnie's chief source at the Yale Library, where she sometimes worked, was a privately published, gossipy memoir, *Society as I Have Found It*, by New Yorker Ward McAllister, who is represented in the novel by both Sillerton Jackson, self-appointed arbiter of social forms, and Lawrence Lefferts, the philandering side of the gossip. Although McAllister's book was useful, Minnie could barely stand to use it. As she writes to Wharton, "'Little did I think I'd ever consult him! . . . such bosh I never tackled.'"[5]

Wharton's letters to Mary Cadwalader Jones show how reciprocal were their efforts on the novel. They both enjoyed the flurry of curiosity brought on by the serial publication of the book; magazine editor Rutger Jewett wrote to Wharton that "'Society (spelled with a capital "S") is trying to fit familiar New York names to your characters.'"[6] Although writing a roman à clef was not Wharton's intention, re-creating the place and age of New York in the 1870s was. She later writes in her autobiography about her "photographic memory of rooms and houses—even those seen but briefly, or at long intervals. . . .

My visual sensibility must always have been too keen for middling pleasures" (*ABG*, 805). Even though she had used well that large accumulation of visual information in her first published book, *The Decoration of Houses*, which she coauthored with architect Ogden Codman, Wharton saw that her vast and somewhat peculiar store of knowledge brought with it responsibility. For instance, after *The Age of Innocence* had been published and dramatist Zoë Akins was writing a screenplay of it, Wharton writes to Minnie about the stage detail she thought would be necessary:

> I am very anxious about the staging & dressing. I could do every stick of furniture & every rag of clothing myself, for every detail of that far-off scene was indelibly stamped on my infant brain. I am so much afraid that the young actors will be "Summit Collar" athletes, with stern jaws & shaven lips, instead of gentlemen. Of course they ought all to have moustaches, & not tooth brush ones, but curved & slightly twisted at the ends. They should wear dark grey frock-coats & tall hats, & always buttonhole-violets by day, a gardenia in evening dress. White waistcoats with their evening clothes, & pumps, I think. But you will remember all this as well as I do. . . .[7]

The real impetus for Wharton's writing *The Age of Innocence* was less her fascination with a "lost" age than it was her desire to reaffirm many of the cultural values she had, in 1919, come to see as "lost." The cataclysmic devastation of the Great War had not only isolated her from America, it had convinced her—perhaps necessarily—of the inherent madness of all civilization: any kind of destruction could be justified once a culture abandoned basic human principles. She recalls in her autobiography that even though she had early on considered "the group in which I grew up . . . like an empty vessel into which no new wine would ever again be poured," she had been too harsh. In this postwar time she had come to see that "one of its uses lay in preserving a few drops of an old vintage too rare to be savoured by a youthful palate; and I should like to atone for my unappreciativeness by trying to revive that faint fragrance" (*ABG*, 780). Behind Wharton's change of heart lay her belief that during the 1870s "the Americans of the original States, who in moments of crisis still shaped the national point of view, were the heirs of an old tradition of European culture which the country has now totally rejected." The continuum of human values, then, which had remained in place during the 1870s and 1880s, had by 1914 been disrupted—in the United States as well as in Europe. What had replaced these decades of humane values, to Wharton's dismay, was a shrill enthusiasm for "telephones, motors, electric light, central heating, X-rays, cinemas, radium, aeroplanes and wireless telegraphy"[8] (781)—superficial products of modern times that had no bearing on moral principle.

Edith Wharton needed Minnie's help partly because she had very little time to do any research herself. She was in need of money after her costly war relief efforts of the previous four years. She was also hard hit by the low prices paid for her writing during the war years and, as a United States citizen, by the new federal income taxes and the vicissitudes of stock and property values. So when Appleton Publishers offered to serialize her "New York" novel in *Pictorial Review,* she hurried to accept the terms. The novel, however, had to be written very quickly—between late summer of 1919 and March of 1920. It was a herculean task, but one Wharton felt was essential—to both her financial and her emotional well-being.

Wharton's method of writing was more professional than it was dramatic: she did not isolate herself from people in order to plunge into the lives of her characters. Rather, she carefully compartmentalized her time so that she continued to lead what appeared to be a busy social life even during her most intensely creative periods. She was always precise about her responsibilities, and when she heard a rumor that *Pictorial Review* was going to cut her manuscript (on the premise that she wrote long novels, and readers preferred short ones), she wrote immediately to Rutger Jewett, declaring that "as I am prepared to keep my part of the agreement I shall expect the Magazine to do the same and not to tamper with the text of my novel." She continues, "I have done really a super-human piece of work in writing, within a year, the best part of two long novels, entirely different in subject and treatment, simply to suit the convenience of the Editor of the Pictorial, and I cannot consent to have my work treated as if it were prose-by-the-yard."[9]

Her stand was reasonable. She wrote and rewrote, first writing sections and then rewriting from the typed versions of this material prepared by her secretary. The process was multilayered, with several sets of rewritten chapters leading to her beginning the next section again in handwriting. Once she had designed a book, with chapters planned to cover this part of the narrative or that, she could not interrupt her writing process to cut lines of exposition or story. And besides, as her sometimes acerbic comments show, Wharton was very clear about her rationale for doing what she did—the beautifully fused plot and character development make up the skeleton of her fiction. As she comments in both *The Writing of Fiction* and her autobiography, the birth of any story idea is a miracle. There is no consistency or predictability.

> In the birth of fiction, it is sometimes the situation, the "case," which first presents itself, and sometimes the characters who appear, asking to be fitted into a situation. It is hard to say what conditions are likely to give the priority to one or the other, and I doubt if fiction can be usefully divided into novels of situation and of character, since a novel, if worth anything at all, is always both, in inextricable combination. (*ABG*, 935)

Wharton's sense of this magic was one of her ties to the young modernists, and she frequently balked at having to explain the writing process. She was seldom at a loss for topics and themes, but she denied that she did much rational planning at the early stages of a work. In this comment from her memoir, she wreaks havoc with the programmed, structured approach to writing fiction: "The truth is that I have never attached much importance to subject, partly because every incident, every situation, presents itself to me in the light of story-telling material, and partly from the conviction that the possibilities of a given subject are—whatever a given imagination can make of them" (*ABG*, 934). Reminiscent of Henry James's prefaces, Wharton's remarks place her in the camp of those artists who are not afraid of inspiration, or at least of admitting that they welcome it.

Edith Wharton's View of The Age of Innocence

Some aspects of her writing were not solitary, however. In the case of *The Age of Innocence,* she turned to her longtime friend, the critic Walter Berry, for his reading of and advice about her manuscript. Because he had also been part of the 1870s and 1880s New York scene, Berry was as moved as Wharton by her re-creation of the times. He warned her, however, that the two of them were "the only people who will ever read it. We are the last people left who can remember New York and Newport as they were then, and nobody else will be interested" (*ABG,* 1056–57). Although Wharton secretly agreed with Berry, she knew that her descriptions of the societies were interesting chiefly as backdrops for the real narrative, the love story. She confesses in a December 1920 letter to a friend, "I did so want 'The Age' to be taken not as a 'costume piece' but as a 'simple & grave' story of two people trying to live up to something that was still 'felt in the blood' at that time."[10]

There is little question that many elements of Wharton's 1920 novel are autobiographical. Even her habitual reliance on Walter Berry's opinion bore some relation to the narrative as autobiography: Berry had been her suitor in Bar Harbor, Maine, in 1883, the summer after her engagement to Harry Stevens had been broken through the interference of his mother. When Berry, who was at the time a young lawyer chronically ill with the effects of malaria, and hardly wealthy, left without proposing to her, Edith Jones was bewildered. Later that summer, Teddy Wharton, a friend of her older brother's, began courting her. Wharton was 13 years Edith's senior. Amiable, pleasure-loving, and from a reasonably wealthy family, the Bostonian was considered a suitable match, and the two were married in the spring of 1885. Unfortunately, the strain of mental illness in the Wharton family would soon surface. (Berry never married, but he was much admired and moved in the same circles as Edith and Teddy Wharton.)[11]

By 1919, when Wharton began writing *The Age of Innocence,* Berry had been her close friend for nearly 25 years. Neither of them believed in those traditional values so dominant in 19th-century New York; for one thing, in 1913 Wharton had divorced her husband of more than a quarter century. Sadly, the New York society of her parents and friends found it difficult to accept a divorced woman, even though Teddy's manic and aggressive behavior had been evident for a decade. So Edith Wharton moved to Paris. (In fact, she returned to the United States only once more in her lifetime, in 1923, to accept an honorary degree given to her—a woman who had never attended any college—by Yale University.) It was from the perspective of an expatriate, then, a person living primarily in a country not her own, that Wharton looked back on the years of her childhood, years when both America—and the author—were much more innocent.

Was this what Wharton had in mind when she titled the novel about a classic romantic triangle—a man bewilderingly "in love" with two very different women—*The Age of Innocence*? The glimpse back to a time when a pledge to marry held, even if a passion for another gripped one of the engaged pair? The scene of modest reserve when the bride-to-be offers her lover his freedom, but for the wrong reasons? The relinquishment of an all-absorbing love for a dull, steady one? Or does the title gently ridicule the culture of the 1870s that insisted its daughters lead such sheltered and circumspect lives that no passion would ever touch them? How protected, how innocent, can a woman in love remain? How much control can a society have over any human being?

Another factor that influenced the way Wharton wrote this novel was that by the time she returned imaginatively to her childhood, she was in her late 50s. She had been an eminently successful novelist for more than 20 years, and she had learned that she preferred as friends those rich in learning and the arts, such as the American novelist Henry James, rather than those who were financially wealthy. Having seen the falsity of some parts of a society determined only by wealth, Wharton was hardly likely to deify the rich in her fictionalized New York.

The most pressing reason for Wharton to write this complex love story, however, may have been a subconscious one. A significant part of her past that fed into the book was her 1908–10 love affair with American journalist Morton Fullerton. For various reasons, Wharton's marriage had been sexually unsatisfying: she and Teddy seldom had intercourse, and there were no children. So when (23 years into her marriage) she fell in love in all senses of the word, the liaison with a man not her husband reaffirmed her womanliness, both physically and emotionally. Unfortunately, the affair was brief, and Edith's poignant letters to Fullerton reveal subsequent years of heartbreak.[12] Fullerton had had—and continued to have—many sex partners, and Wharton's passion for the young man was, in some ways, unreturned. What the relationship provided for Wharton as writer, however, was the emotive power that shaped *The Age of Innocence.* Her own passion colored the torment of all three of her fictional characters—Newland Archer, Ellen Olenska, and even May Welland.

The novel tells the story of would-be lovers caught in a wealthy, self-scrutinizing, and self-satisfied society. During the 1870s, what the members of New York's elite think of each other is more important than individual effort, honor, or happiness. And although Wharton shows clearly that some members of society's upper echelon are hypocrites (secretly participating in the very acts they criticize others for considering), most lead the lives they deem suitable for people in their positions. They are true gentlemen and ladies; there is no pretense to their identities.

In Wharton's planning notebook, however, she says little about the novel being a picture of New York society. It is clear that the narrative was to be more a story of troubled—and unfulfilled—romance than an anatomy of that "age" the title suggests. According to her notes, the plot involved a young man from a "very good 'Old New York'" family; his fiancée from the same kind of family; and her older cousin, returning to the United States after an unhappy marriage to a Polish count.[13]

Ethnic identification would have signaled Wharton's readers that the cousin, Ellen Olenska, by marrying into Polish society, had corrupted herself—perhaps beyond saving. The issue would have been not only her divorce (had the family allowed her to divorce the count), but her years of immersion in what British and American readers suspected was rampant Polish immorality. This ethnic coding suggests that Newland Archer's attempts to reclaim Ellen, to draw her back into moral American society, are doomed to fail.

Readers' attention fell on Archer partly because it was rare for serious novels to have women protagonists. (Traditionally, the novel privileged male experience, in the form of either adventurous heroes or men maturing through education. Obviously, opportunities for 19th-century women to have either adventures or educations were infrequent, and therefore implausible.) Wharton reinforced her readers' expectations by opening the novel with descriptions of Archer as he muses about his choice of the innocent May Welland as his bride-to-be. The reader comes to know Newland first: Wharton gives him center stage.

He remains the center of attention throughout the novel. As the narrative progresses, Newland's is the active dilemma. He must make the choices: whether or not to continue courting May; whether or not to marry her; whether or not to woo Ellen (sending her yellow roses is the beginning of this formal courtship). After Newland marries May, in a scene touchingly poignant in its hollowness, his decisions continue: whether or not to see Ellen; whether or not to set up Ellen as his mistress; whether or not to divorce May; whether or not to abandon her and go to Europe to live with Ellen. Ironically, the only act Newland accomplishes is that of marrying May, and in that act he has the support—and the complicity—of his entire culture. Wharton suggests that without this overwhelming approval, Archer would continue to live in the fantasy world he finds in his books, his daydreams, and his idealizations of what "life" is meant to be. That he might act on his own—against odds, and against social mandates—would be unlikely.

Wharton's genius in creating Newland Archer is that she does not make him evil, selfish, or even careless. He falls into double standard behavior so unconsciously that his love of Ellen seems only right. It goes along unquestioned by the reader (who becomes guilty of approving of the double standard in the process of wanting Newland and Ellen to become lovers)—until the brilliant scene in the carriage when Ellen voices the real conflict: "we'll look, not at visions, but at realities. . . . Is it your idea, then, that I should live with you as your mistress—since I can't be your wife?" (289). After the words are said, Archer himself has to react to them. Sadly, in a later scene, his defense is to impugn Ellen rather than take the blame himself: "'She'll come!'

he said to himself, almost contemptuously" (309). Even though he has made the suggestion that they become lovers, even though he is the married man, he slips into the male attitude of censuring the woman who is willing to love him.

That Wharton grappled with the behavior of this idealistic, seemingly honest man is evidenced by the three plot variations in her notebook. Archer, caught in the social codes of the 1870s, is a mystery. What would be plausible behavior for such a man? In one of the plots, Ellen and Archer escape from their society and try out romance. Although Ellen is happy with their illicit passion, Newland cannot forget the culture in which he has been reared. Wharton writes, "He cannot live without New York and respectability, nor she without Europe and emotion" (quoted in Price, 26). In another version, they marry but Ellen later leaves him for life in Europe: her soul "recoils" at the sameness of his American existence. In a third, they spend "a few mad weeks" together in Florida, but Newland cannot imagine living publicly with Ellen (being Catholic, she cannot divorce the count), and she, for her part, "is weary of their sentimental tête à tête and his scruples" (quoted in Price, 27). In this plot, as in the second, the family cooperates subtly to send Ellen back to Europe, complete with a farewell dinner.

One reason Wharton chose the latter narrative outcome was that by doing so she could valorize the claim of wife and mother, all the while showing society's willingness to sacrifice one of its own (to, in effect, dismember itself) in order to protect family values. Her censure of New York society dominates the plot early on. In the powerful scenes of the group's acquiescence to maintaining order—whether they are in Mrs. Manson Mingott's bedroom or in the Archers' or the van der Luydens' dining rooms—the reader sees that the social group is of one mind, one heart. If Ellen will insist on being different and difficult, if she will give up her fortune to the Polish count rather than live with him on her own terms, then she must be cast out. Her independence threatens the stability of old New York.

It seems clear that Edith Wharton—a successful and comparatively wealthy woman writer—felt the same sense of alienation she creates for Ellen Olenska. Threatening to the family and friends who remained in New York and Newport, the prominent American novelist (herself living abroad) explores both passion and its renunciation in what would become her most significant novel. And by never providing readers with Ellen Olenska's full story, Wharton maintains the kind of dignified silence that was customary for her, a woman recognizable as a product of "the age of innocence."

5

The Age of Innocence as Ironic "Novel of Manners"

If categorizing Wharton's novel as one of manners preserved it, made it a standard choice in that genre, then using the phrase to describe it was useful. It was also a trap. Readers during the mid-20th century were more interested in avant-garde, highly experimental fiction—the American modernists' work—or the proletarian novels of the 1930s, with their clear social messages. A "novel of manners" suggested dullness, a story privileging setting and decor over interaction among characters.

The novel of manners in American letters as defined by James Tuttleton, however, is not necessarily boring: "a novel in which the manners, social customs, folkways, conventions, traditions, and mores of a given social group . . . play a dominant role in the lives of fictional characters, exert control over their thought and behavior." Furthermore, these manners and customs, in the fictional representation, are detailed with "a premium upon the exactness of the representation."[1] Readers the world over had appreciated the attention to mores and morals in the greatest works of Balzac, Flaubert, Dostoevsky, Dickens, Austen, and many others; the form was thought to be sophisticated and largely Continental.

Wharton read a great deal of Continental literature, which she admired more than she did much literature in English. She was surely familiar with the conventions of the form; and by her own account, *The Age of Innocence* was infused with as much exact detail as she could remember or unearth. Her point in using that detail, however, went much further than any superficial "accuracy." Wharton was writing about characters she saw as both informed and stifled by their observance of correct social forms. The tragedy of the Archers, the Wellands, and their friends would be incomprehensible to readers without information about how the forms and codes governed their behavior. Readers need to know, at least, that the polite response to existing codes in 1870s New York was obedience. If one differed from the expected behavior, the culture was perplexed: what were the motives of anyone who did not abide by social codes? With threat came fear. For causing fear, a person could be punished, perhaps even ostracized or exiled.

In the days when sociology was a young discipline and anthropology an exotic one, the conventions of a novel of manners might have needed some explaining. Today, most readers would hope that a major work of fiction would include at least some cultural impressions. Few characters, even the most complex or introspective ones, can hold a reader's interest in the 1990s for a substantial period of time; we tend to agree with Lionel Trilling's notion that the best fiction should reflect "a culture's hum and buzz of implication" (6).

Early in the 20th century, some critics objected to the use of this genre for American fiction, claiming that because the United States was not a "classed" society (as England or India were seen to be), an author could not focus on differences of cultural strata. But, as Tuttleton notes, so long as the society under scrutiny is comprised of groups "with recognizable and differentiable manners and conventions" (10), an author can derive a clear focus. The chief responsibility of the novelist of manners is to show readers the classes or segments of society, and what mores govern them.

Although Wharton worked very hard to depict cultures composed of separate, identifiable strands in *The House of Mirth* and *The Fruit of the Tree,* in which she uses occupational differences to distinguish her characters, her aim in *The Age of Innocence* is more subtle. Her 1920 novel is about a culture under attack (perhaps reasonably so) from within, rather than from without. *The House of Mirth* shows the bastions of achieved society being scaled by any number of nouveaux riches; part of the cohesion of the upper classes in that novel grows from the need to resist invasion by the Gormers, the Wellington Brys, and Sim Rosedale.

In *The Age of Innocence,* Wharton paints a portrait of a society fighting different battles. In this work, society is able to maintain its calm facade because few people are audacious enough to try to enter the closed upper class; rather, the problems that fuel the novel come from those class members who are already accepted. Although Larry Lefferts seems to be a paragon of respectability, for example, much of one secondary plot focuses on the tactics he hopes will disguise his illicit affairs. Wharton's irony is doubly effective because she makes Lefferts one of the monitors of the social code: the reader meets him first talking about—and judging—Ellen Olenska.

> "Well—upon my soul!" exclaimed Lawrence Lefferts, turning his opera-glass abruptly away from the stage. Lawrence Lefferts was, on the whole, the foremost authority on "form" in New York. He had probably devoted more time than any one else to the study of this intricate and fascinating question. . . . "My God!" he said; and silently handed his glass to old Sillerton Jackson. (8–9)

After describing the object of the men's scrutiny, Ellen Olenska sitting in the Wellands' box, Wharton focuses on Jackson's returning the opera-glass to Lefferts, with the authorial comment, "The whole of the club turned instinctively, waiting to hear what the old man had to say; for old Mr. Jackson was as great an authority on 'family' as Lawrence Lefferts was on 'form'" (9).

Much of this early chapter works to establish the power of achieved social authority. Wharton prefaces the scene with a short meditation on the fact that even the free-thinking Archer is a part of such "masculine solidarity," used to accepting "their doctrine on all the issues called moral. He instinctively felt that in this respect it would be troublesome—and also rather bad form—to strike out for himself" (8). The structure of the novel hammers home this point: Lefferts, Jackson, and their clique decide that Ellen's being at the opera, given the scandal of her having left an abusive husband, is improper. Archer, who seldom acts and here does not disagree with his friends, leaves them to go to the Wellands' box. Wharton spells out plainly how unusual such action is for Archer. She also underscores the power of the men's judgment.

In the following scene, when Newland is introduced to Ellen, Wharton draws the sophisticated European woman as a naïf. She has been gone too long; she no longer understands the social forms. Archer feels a pang of worried concern for her, particularly as he knows that the people she views as kindly are judging her—in Wharton's words, "trying her case"—that very moment (17). With diligent detail, Wharton makes plain that the New York men wielding their influence know nothing about Ellen, or her marital situation, or her life, or her means. What they see in the opera box—a lovely woman in a dark blue velvet gown, her hair styled in a "Josephine look"—is the full extent of their information.

In another secondary plot, more dominant because it pits Newland Archer against a character readers would consider unsavory, Julius Beaufort—the symbol of the unconventional "new" man—lives a life without honor, scruple, or care. Because he has married the well-born Regina Dallas, Beaufort is almost accepted. His profession as banker, however, creates some distaste for his wealth (that his house has the only actual ballroom in town compensates for his moral insta-bility), as does his all-too-public affair with his mistress, Fanny Ring. Sillerton Jackson sums up society's disapproval when he says, "'Certain nuances escape Beaufort.'" Newland's mother agrees, and adds the force of still earlier generations:

> "Oh, necessarily; Beaufort is a vulgar man," said Mrs. Archer. "My grandfather Newland always used to say to my mother: 'Whatever you do, don't let that fellow Beaufort be introduced to the girls.'" (35)

The Age of Innocence *as Ironic "Novel of Manners"*

Wharton's use of dramatic irony here is far-reaching. Although the author implies that everyone understands Beaufort's tenuous place in society, nothing is ever said to that effect. So when Beaufort begins to escort Ellen Olenska home from shopping or a walk, she has no idea his attentions should be suspect. What are the signs? Beaufort sends her flowers, but so does Newland, as well as the scion of New York society, Henry van der Luyden.

Ellen is often with Beaufort when Archer wants to see her, and the juxtaposition is always jarring to Archer. He wants Ellen to understand how dangerous Beaufort's attentions are, but he cannot bring himself to warn her. In the gap, and convinced of Newland's frustration, the reader supplies the unspoken dialogue. And then Wharton writes a scene delightful in its irony, as Ellen links Beaufort and Newland as two men capable of helping her understand New York customs:

> "There are only two people here who make me feel as if they understood what I mean and could explain things to me: you and Mr. Beaufort." Archer winced at the joining of the names, and then, with a quick readjustment, understood, sympathised, and pitied. (76)

What Wharton's narrative crossings impart to the reader— beyond a sense of Ellen's innocence—is that Newland's motives are every bit as suspect as Julius's. The greatest of ironies is that months will pass before Newland is honest with himself. He loves Ellen, not May.

Even though the denouement of the novel includes Beaufort's financial disaster as one of its threads, there is still a reservoir of sympathy for the man Wharton tries to draw as immoral. For in the whole scheme of social interaction, Beaufort is at least reasonably honest about his life, his appearances, and his dealings. That he is a banker saves him from what might have been an unforgivable flaw—his financial dealings. As Wharton reminisces in her memoir, "The Schermerhorns, Joneses, Pendletons, on my father's side, the Stevenses, Ledyards, Rhinelanders on my mother's, the Gallatins on both, seem all to have belonged to the same prosperous class of merchants, bankers and lawyers. It was a society from which all dealers in retail business were excluded as a matter of course" (*ABG*, 784).

In contrast to Beaufort, socially acceptable men who appear to be above suspicion, even as they are leading reprehensible lives, fall below Beaufort in Wharton's hierarchy of respectability. The most despicable of the group are those who understand the code so well that they can do exactly as they please without appearing to break rules. Using the conventions for their own pleasure, they define themselves as being, in effect, above the law.

Ellen Olenska is no businessperson, but she is as much an outsider as Beaufort. Wharton creates a set of differences for her that loom large in the eyes of New York's elite. In part, her differences excuse some of her questionable behavior. Wharton here uses that device from the traditional novel of manners, describing characters from enough different groups that levels of kinds of behavior can exist. From the beginning of *The Age of Innocence*, Ellen is the exotic "foreign" child. When she first comes to New York at nine or 10, after "a roaming babyhood" at the hands of her parents (whom Wharton calls "continental wanderers"), people are attracted by her strange skills— doing Spanish dances and speaking languages other than English. An orphan in the care of her eccentric aunt, the Marchioness Manson, whose career consists of moving from one marriage to another as she drops down the social ladder (a movement signaled by her buying smaller and smaller houses whenever she returns to New York), Ellen has no hope of a stable, proper home life. Medora Manson is a wanderer, too, so Ellen soon returns to Europe; there she marries Count Olenski.

New York can, then, partly excuse Ellen: she has not grown up surrounded by propriety; she has had no way to learn the rules. But society's tolerance is undermined from the start because Ellen seems disinterested in learning these rules, and once she has been in New York a while, instead of learning them, seems intent on going her own way. She lives in an artistic area (a "strange quarter") rather than with her relatives; she likes writers, painters, and actresses, and is as comfortable at Mrs. Struthers' Sunday evenings as at acceptable places.

The Age of Innocence *as Ironic "Novel of Manners"*

Even the furnishings in her rented house suggest the intimate and the "foreign" (70). Wharton makes clear that Ellen needs instruction, that the cultural maze she tries to navigate in New York is more peculiar, and dangerous, than such situations in the countries of Europe.

In order to convey how prejudiced New York society is toward Europe (and consequently toward Ellen, in its categorization of her as "foreign"), Wharton draws comparisons within the narrative. Newland and May, following the conventions of their class and age, go abroad on their honeymoon. In contrast to Newland's early romantic vision of taking May to the idyllic Italian lakes, where they can read poetry and enjoy each other, the newlyweds instead spend their weeks shopping for Paris gowns for May. They also avoid all contact with the inhabitants—and the cultures—of the countries they visit.

May's near phobia about remaining isolated from those cultures—even in England, where there is no language barrier—is another mark of her proper upbringing. Wharton recalls in her autobiography, "It was thought vulgar and snobbish to try to make the acquaintance, in London, Paris or Rome, of people of the class corresponding to their own. The Americans who forced their way into good society in Europe were said to be those who were shut out from it at home; and the self-respecting American on his travels frequented only the little 'colonies' of his compatriots already settled in the European capitals, and only their most irreproachable members! What these artless travellers chiefly enjoyed were scenery, ruins and historic sites . . . and the shops!" (*ABG*, 831–32).

In the novel, Wharton calls attention to this senseless American behavior by building the honeymoon weeks around a London dinner invitation. Newland and May's being invited to dine by a friend of Mrs. Archer sparks one of their rare arguments. May, worried over what to wear, pouts and complains she finds intellectual conversations boring. She also does not want to put herself out (to dress splendidly) for a modest, middle-class occasion.

Once at the dinner (which is, indeed, modest), Newland meets a young French tutor he finds interesting—fluent, well-educated, perceptive. When he later suggests to May that they entertain M. Rivière, she is horrified. "'The little Frenchman? Wasn't he dreadfully common?' she asks, looking at Newland strangely" (202). Wharton's artistry makes clear that May's taste—and her motivation—is very different from Newland's. For all her foreign travel, May remains firmly "New York," complete with her society's extreme class consciousness, and Newland's early dream of educating her crumbles repeatedly during their travels. In this scene, with Newland's admiration for M. Rivière so clear, Wharton brings the narrative of Newland and Ellen back into focus. For Rivière is Count Olenski's former secretary, the man who helped Ellen escape her husband, the man rumored to have been her lover. In a single scene, Wharton manages to both complicate the plot and draw a number of characters definitively, giving the reader new insights into the seemingly naive May, a woman less malleable once married than she appears to be during her engagement.

Like Henry James's *The American* and *The Ambassadors, The Age of Innocence* makes a series of complex statements about cultures and nationalities, as well as the stereotypes that accrue from the failure to investigate the realities of both. Wharton's scrutiny of national character, and the constructions people place on that kind of definition, moves her novel of manners into the category Tuttleton describes as subversive. He points out that some writers of novels of manners are intrigued primarily with capturing the times and the culture, while others use the narrative form to prepare readers for an "ideological argument" (10). Surely, one of Wharton's aims was to prove to American readers, who bought most of her books, that their fears of Europe were unfounded, that culture abroad was no more threatening, and no more "foreign," than many segments of culture within the United States. To isolate Ellen Olenska because of her European childhood or her marriage to a Polish man made no sense at all.

The subversive quality of this theme shows itself in Wharton's ability to write scenes that counterpoint each other, drawing the reader into the full text of the book through his or her own reading. For example, following the scene in which May denigrates Newland's friendship with the French tutor, Wharton moves immediately back to the United States, to the triumphal scene of the innocent but deadly May winning the Newport Archery Club contest.

The Age of Innocence *as Ironic "Novel of Manners"*

In the midst of "scarlet geranium and coleus, and cast-iron vases painted in chocolate colour," two large targets are erected (204), and there May—described often as the huntress Diana—wins her diamond-tipped arrow pin for marksmanship. Wharton drew the vivid scene from her childhood memories of those apparent "young gods and goddesses" (*ABG*, 819), heavily veiled but fully intent on their pursuits:

> She had her bow and arrow in her hand, and placing herself on the chalk-mark traced on the turf she lifted the bow to her shoulder and took aim. The attitude was so full of a classic grace that a murmur of appreciation followed her appearance. . . . Her rivals—Mrs. Reggie Chivers, the Merry girls, and divers rosy Thorleys, Dagonets and Mingotts, stood behind her in a lovely anxious group, brown heads and golden bent above the scores, and pale muslins and flower-wreathed hats mingled in a tender rainbow. (211)

Replete with innuendo about May's still virginal charm, the scene is inscribed with acerbity. Like Diana, May knows exactly what she is capable of winning, and in her scale of values, the archery contest is only another means of proving herself superior to Ellen. When she insists that they have time before dinner to show her grandmother, Catherine Mingott, the prize—guessing that Ellen has spent the day there—Newland goes along unsuspectingly. Rather than his being in control of events, it is his young wife who is aware—and armed.

6

The Age of Innocence as Ironic "Traditional" Novel

There are a number of fictional formats in addition to the novel of manners that Wharton might have chosen to replicate. A successful author for 20 years, she had written novels of character, of marriage, of class, and even of intrigue. She had published as many ghost stories as she had sentimental tales; increasingly, however, as she grew more sure of her craft, Wharton avoided this last category. Although she could appreciate some fiction by Sarah Orne Jewett and Mary Wilkins Freeman, the mature Wharton most decidedly avoided writing "local color" or "regional" fiction.[1]

In the turn-of-the-century American enthusiasm for realistic narrative, writers as different as Kate Chopin, Bret Harte, Alice Cary, Stephen Crane, Ambrose Bierce, Jewett and Freeman were called "local color" writers because their fiction attempted to draw the life of people living in a particular place. Chopin's Creole characters, complete with a French patois, like Harte's Western cowboy characters, led readers to distance themselves from the fiction. In the case of the many women writers who wrote about small town life in New England, a kind of homey domestic fiction came to represent that brand of regional or local writing. Calm on the surface, such fiction often described inequities of race or gender; all too often, however, local color was considered quaint, and Wharton wanted no part of it.

Had she not worked carefully, her earlier novellas—*Ethan Frome* and *Summer,* both set in poverty-crippled New England villages—would surely have been categorized as regional writing, filled with the type of local-color details Freeman and Jewett were famous for. But the purposeful and undeniable tragedies of both books infused them with pathos rather than the complacent reassurance usually found in women's local-color writing.

Judith Fryer coined the term "urban pastoral" to describe much of Wharton's fiction. Acknowledging that the author drew social scenes carefully, Fryer points out that Wharton never liked the country, which she saw as desolate and destroying. Her province was the city, and the upper circles of city dwellers; yet within that urban setting, she chose themes and events that could be used to create a pastoral sense of tranquillity. Fryer defines "pastoral" as privilege, as a place that is itself privileged, idyllic. Rather than finding such terrain in nature, as poets often did, Wharton found that space in the morally secure enclaves of truly civilized cultures.[2]

The chief distinction between New England local color and Wharton's urban pastoral was the latter's careful selectivity. Instead of realistic and sometimes random detail, Wharton chose to describe what she considered culturally significant objects and interactions, letting her work convey a stable moral message. The performances of men and women in the elite social circles of *The Age of Innocence* are weighted with meaning: Newland's presenting himself in the Welland box is a protective gesture, a joining of his family influence with the Wellands' and the Mingotts' in order to defend the propriety of Ellen Olenska's attending the opera. His urging the Wellands to announce his and May's engagement is a parallel gesture.

In this novel particularly, Wharton is concerned with the social forms having to do with courtship and marriage. Therefore, to most readers, *The Age of Innocence* is an example of the 19th-century marriage novel. (The source of stability for much late Victorian society remained the social arrangement based on marriage, lines of descent, legitimacy.) The marriage novel ends with either the proposal or the wedding of characters whose lives seem devoted to finding the ideal mate. Even when it looked as if Wharton might be writing such a novel, she often gave such a work a narrative far removed from any simple drive toward the perfect melding of man and woman.

In *The Age of Innocence,* for example, rather than have the text culminate with Newland and May's marriage, Wharton divides the work into two books. In the first, which seems to have a relatively conventional marriage plot, Newland becomes engaged to May and then begs her to set an early wedding date. Although she guesses that he is infatuated with her cousin, Ellen, she pretends to think he remains involved with his married lover—and under that guise offers him his freedom. The plot here rises to this anticipated "break" but quickly falls back into the marriage plot. Wharton's disruption of the expected happy ending (the wedding) occurs at the end of Book One, as Newland laughs hysterically when he receives May's telegram agreeing to the early date. Ironically, in the three days since he pleaded with her to set a spring date, he and the Countess Olenska have admitted their love for each other. Now he is caught in a wedding planned for less than a month away, with no hope of breaking his betrothal.

Book Two opens with the marriage ceremony itself, "a rite that seemed to belong to the dawn of history" (179), one that Ellen is not present to see. In the gaping space between Newland's mad laughter and his deadly calm acquiescence the morning of the wedding lies enough material for another book. Wharton's complete omission of any description of the last weeks of freedom for both Newland and May creates a structure that avoids the usual subject of the marriage novel—the states of mind of the couple during their last prenuptial days.

Her omission is ominous. If the reader must be shielded from Newland's possible angst, there is no reason to avoid May's jubilance. The utter silence about both people warns the reader away: the blank space between Books One and Two inscribes an unspeakable narrative, leading the reader to believe that this wedding ceremony should never have taken place.

The Age of Innocence *as Ironic "Traditional" Novel*

Book Two opens with Newland's cynical introspection:

"And all the while, I suppose," he thought, "real people were living somewhere, and real things happening to them . . ." (182)

He pretends to himself that, without Ellen, nothing matters. Saying his vows, holding May's hands, he continues his grimly silent soliloquy: "suddenly the same black abyss yawned before him and he felt himself sinking into it, deeper and deeper, while his voice rambled on smoothly and cheerfully" (187).

Wharton's narrative strategy makes *The Age of Innocence* no simple marriage novel. By putting Newland Archer at the center of the text, Wharton shifts the reader's attention to that most traditional novel form, the quest (or the younger male variant of it, the novel of education or bildungsroman). The author's signal that this is at least in part a book about male self-exploration and self-discovery is her allusions to the Faust legend in the early scenes.

If one reads Newland as a Faust figure—hungry for knowledge, superior to his peers, set on changing his existence—then the initial exposition in the novel, as Newland both scrutinizes his culture and meditates on his and May's role in it, carries double weight. It helps place Newland in the venerable tradition of "man who seeks knowledge."[3] Continuing this paradigm, May becomes Faust's Margaret, the epitome of innocence; and Ellen becomes the Martha of Goethe's drama. But whereas Goethe pits innocence against experience in an oppositional format, Wharton embroiders this duality with heavy irony. Margaret's pregnancy dooms her and leads to the murder of her child, to her incarceration and madness. May's, in contrast, leads to her most obvious act of manipulation—her telling Ellen that she is pregnant so that the would-be lovers' plans for a tryst are aborted. May knows only triumph.

For all his intellectual intentions, Newland fails to learn much beyond his own narrow boundaries of romantic texts. While Faust risks both present-day life and eternal existence in his quest, Newland risks nothing. The tentative formulation of his relationship with Ellen shows his cowardice, just as the ending shows his reluctance to put anything of his—illusions as well as reputation—in danger. While Newland experiences a Walpurgis Night before his marriage, he avoids any kind of sensual physical involvement after it (bolting from the carriage, touching only Ellen's hands).

The imagery of the novel, which is in some ways melodramatic for Wharton, also suggests Faustian concerns. Ellen calls the world of New York "heaven." Similarly, Newland describes Ellen's existence with the count (about which he knows little) as "hell." He sees himself as his wife's "soul's custodian," while May is described as being his "possession." All these terms echo the scenes in *Faust* in which Mephistopheles tempts Faust and is abetted in his design by Wagner, the true innocent. Although Faust has more insight than his younger protégé, it is May who becomes the more knowledgeable of the Archers. The tribal farewell dinner, a rite of sacrifice, shows May victorious and Newland only bewildered.

The close of *The Age of Innocence* gives us Newland as Faust, an aging character now professing a belief in faith, hope, and patience, yet doing so, in reality, to save his own life. Wharton makes clear that it is Ellen—in her delight in living for the moment—who assumes the Faustian quest. It is also fitting that Newland's moment of decision—whether or not to marry May—takes place at Easter, the Christian anniversary of rebirth, and the point in *Faust* when Heaven's voices occur. That Newland does not "make" that decision, but only accepts May's decision in the telegram, places him even more firmly in the Faustian pattern. Circumstances are Newland's Mephistopheles, and circumstances are often just the machinations of the Welland/Archer tribe.

For Newland, the journey through life seems to have been anything but triumphant. He continues to exist, but by walking away from meeting Ellen, he underscores the futility that has marked much of his 57 years.

And yet, when we read Louis Auchincloss's criticism of Newland—"burstingly complacent . . . as fatuous a young man as one could conceive of"[4]—we want to defend the character. It is less Newland's being at fault than it is the shape of the novel that leaves us surprised at its ending; Wharton's structure emphasizes the lack of conventional resolution. Whether the reader expects a happy ending to the marriage plot (which would be Newland and Ellen reunited) or a satisfying ending to the Faustian search for wisdom (Newland realizing what constitutes his personal happiness), this ending disappoints.

Wharton intentionally heightens the reader's disappointment in two ways. First, she manipulates our understanding of the novel's form. She seems to recast *The Age of Innocence* as a marriage novel: her focus in the last chapter is on the approaching nuptials of Newland and May's son, Dallas, a child named for Regina Dallas Beaufort after Julius Beaufort's financial disgrace. Just as Ellen risked her reputation to visit Regina in the midst of the bankruptcy scandal, so May and Newland also championed that branch of the family. Ironically, the 26-year-old Dallas's fiancée is the child of Beaufort and his mistress, Fanny Ring. Their union will be the fulfillment of Larry Lefferts' prophecy, made in the penultimate chapter, that "we shall see our children fighting for invitations to swindlers' houses, and marrying Beaufort's bastards" (338). Juxtaposed with Dallas's wedding plans is Dallas's announcement that he has arranged a meeting with Ellen Olenska; naturally, the reader expects happy endings for both Dallas and Newland. With May dead from pneumonia and Newland a widower for several years, his meeting with Ellen seems to be the long-delayed answer to the reader's hopes.

Wharton's expert last chapter, however, includes the rationale for what becomes the failed meeting—failed in that it does not occur. The theme of this epilogue is that dramatic changes have marked the quarter century since May's farewell dinner for Ellen. Wharton counterpoints the new ways and the old, Dallas's forthright aggression and Newland's staid diffidence. Given the visible dynamic of past set against present, the reader places Newland's decision not to see Ellen into the context of the past. It becomes a decision that is, finally, explicable. Arthur Mizener describes the ending as Wharton's "simple and terrible truth, that time will come and take man's love away." It also represents Newland's realization that "love kept apart in memory only, like a relic, is . . . dead beyond revival except as a memory."[5]

What keeps the reader hoping, however, is that Newland's turning away from Ellen's home, and a meeting with her, is not inevitable.

The novel could as easily have included a recognition scene, some pleasant interlude when both man and woman enjoy the sight of each other while understanding that any continuation of their relationship is either impossible or inappropriate. It is also possible that Newland and Ellen would have found the kind of instant realization that had marked their earlier affair—that age had not changed their passion for each other. By keeping her two characters from meeting, however, Wharton has stifled the possibility of what most readers would see as a natural denouement, the reunion of Newland with Ellen Olenska.

The puzzle of why Wharton constructed *The Age of Innocence* as she did has everything to do with her concept of an author's intentionality. Caught, as writers in the early 20th century were, between rigid social rules and the avant-garde artistic movements that privileged innovation, Wharton and others found ways to straddle those conflicting mandates. Knowing that the form of a novel is influenced by social forms, Wharton leads her readers to believe the novel is to be a marriage novel. To criticize the "marriage novel" was to blaspheme against upright society. But as we have seen, at key points in the book, Wharton's structure suggests that criticism might be more appropriate than the blind social acceptance that marks the Welland-Archer behavior.

Any such interrogation of social forms had to be done subtly. Most best-sellers reified the social codes; readers' acceptance of a work was usually dependent on their agreeing with the premises expressed in the work. Wharton knew that her readers in 1920 would believe in the sanctity of Newland and May's marriage, particularly with a child on the way. She knew she could not allow even the Newland-in-love-with-Ellen to break from his marriage. But she also understood that her readers would want him to reunite with Ellen once he was a widower. By denying this reunion, Wharton frustrates the reader, and suggests that *The Age of Innocence* was never a simple marriage novel.

Perhaps the most important part of the enigmatic ending is that Ellen Olenska herself does not appear. Although she knows Archer waits below, she does not come to the window. It is her manservant who is seen on the balcony, drawing the shades as night falls. The reader wonders what her gesture (or, rather, lack of gesture) means, and then concludes that Wharton is showing the mature woman character's pride, her desire to meet Newland now silenced in understanding. This is the man she had loved years before, the man torn between the strictures of social convention and the fury of passion. And with age, that fury has mellowed into an acceptance of the rightness of convention. For Newland had been right all along: Ellen did know him, and his behavior here at the end of the narrative—sadly—is all too characteristic.

7

The Age of Innocence as "Modern" Novel

Wharton's 1920 novel is more modern than traditional because it relies for much of its meaning on readers' reactions. Wharton knows how to provoke readers to supply the intentionally missing segments of her work—scenes, character interactions, insight into characters themselves. Unlike the full descriptions of characters provided by 19th-century novelists, Wharton draws highly selective portraits. For example, she describes how Ellen Olenska looks in the opera box, but she does not give any real account of the abuses Ellen suffered during her marriage. Like the members of the New York society so quick to judge the foreign beauty, the reader is limited to largely superficial information.

The gaps in the reader's information about characters parallel the gaps in Wharton's development of the relationships among them. As we have seen, by using a structure that emphasizes untold parts of stories, Wharton leaves the reader free to imagine the missing narratives. When the reader is left with Newland's ironic laughter upon receiving May's telegram, only to find that the following scene is their wedding (with Ellen conveniently, and conspicuously, absent), the missing parts of the story grow more important than what is told.

Other key gaps occur earlier, once Newland and May are engaged and making their betrothal visits. May's inclusion in the van der Luydens' dinner, for example, which has clearly been set up as a chance for Ellen to talk with Newland, colors the unexpected intimacy of Ellen and Newland's conversation. When Newland goes to tea at the countess's—upon her invitation—and finds Beaufort there, another set of omissions looms large: the reader never knows what the relationship between Ellen and Beaufort is, or what Beaufort intends it to be. Weeks after these intriguing, if frustrating, intimacies for Newland and Ellen, he finds himself chosen by his law firm to convince Ellen that she should not divorce her husband. Not only are the missing weeks left blank (during this time, what is Newland's involvement with his bride-to-be's cousin? With his bride-to-be?), but Wharton blinds the reader to the family's motivation. Why is Ellen advised not to divorce the man who has made her so unhappy? More to the point, why is Newland chosen from a large prestigious legal staff to be Ellen's legal advisor?

In its calculated narrative method, *The Age of Innocence* from the start questions motive in relation to the rhetoric that shrouds it. When Letterblair says to Newland, "'The whole family are against a divorce. And I think rightly'" (97), he links two avenues of immense social pressure. One is professional: Letterblair is the senior partner in the law firm, and Newland is obviously his subordinate. The other is familial: Newland is an outsider to the Mingott family, a group much wealthier and better placed in the society of the times than his own. When Newland asks for permission to talk with Ellen before he decides what his legal advice will be, Letterblair fires back the reality of that family relationship:

> "Mr. Archer, I don't understand you. Do you want to marry into
> a family with a scandalous divorce-suit hanging over it?" (99)

Though Newland pretends a kind of innocence here, he knows all too well that Ellen will have to give up her hope of legally defined freedom. Her family, her society, and her legal staff have all decided that she is to remain the Countess Olenska.

The irony Wharton creates in this scene gives the book a further modernist quality. In Wharton's fictional world, things are frequently not what they seem to be. Even more frequently are they not what they are said to be. Using the theme of personal freedom, Wharton connects this fairly cryptic scene between Letterblair and Newland with the latter's spirited defense of women's intellectual and social freedoms. In an after-dinner conversation with Sillerton Jackson, Newland defends Ellen's right to leave the count, and even to live with the male secretary who helped her escape: "'Who had the right to make her life over if she hadn't? I'm sick of the hypocrisy that would bury alive a woman of her age if her husband prefers to live with harlots. . . . Women ought to be free—as free as we are,' he declared" (41–42).

The enveloping irony of this somewhat idealistic comment is that Newland believes it no more than does Jackson. Both men have seen what their culture does to women who do not keep up the facade of respectability. Wharton's 1905 novel, *The House of Mirth,* tells that specific sad story, as the virginal Lily Bart is condemned out of hand for being beautiful and trusting at age 29. Here, Wharton embeds Newland's real opinions about women's freedoms, particularly their sexual freedoms, in the early sections of the novel.

One of the most telling of Archer's flashbacks is to his affair with the married woman, Mrs. Thorley Rushworth. Despite his sexual relationship with her, he never refers to her by a Christian name: Wharton leaves the reader to imagine the missing scenes of love-making, wondering whether the proper Newland addressed his beloved as "Mrs. Thorley Rushworth" even in the midst of passion. Clearly, much of what attracted the young socialite to that lady was her inaccessibility. Dalliances with married women were safe.

There is nothing romantic—or even polite—about Newland's memories of his affair with the woman he calls his "poor silly" lover. He explains the liaison as only an adventure, one that was his right because his partner was, in fact, "'that kind of woman': foolish, vain, clandestine by nature, and far more attracted by the secrecy and peril of the affair than by such charms and qualities as he possessed" (95). Changing the tone of the situation, however, one of his earlier memories describes Mrs. Rushworth's "frailty which had so nearly marred that unhappy being's life, and had disarranged his own plans for a whole winter" (7). Their two-year affair, and her evident breakdown because of it, is charted as inconvenience rather than tragedy.

For Newland, as for other men of his class, there is an "abysmal distinction between the women one loved and respected and those one enjoyed—and pitied" (96). May Welland belongs in the former category, Mrs. Rushworth in the latter. One of the lingering narrative questions in *The Age of Innocence* is where Ellen Olenska falls in Newland's oversimplified schema.

To make clear how ambivalent Newland is about Ellen—how easily he would relegate her to Mrs. Rushworth's classification—Wharton opens the following scene with his careful notice of her improprieties. Newland visits her at home in order to discuss the possibility of divorce. Not only is he offended by the location of her house (in the artists' quarter), and its furnishings (something intimate, "foreign"), but he finds Julius Beaufort already there (70). In Beaufort's presence, Ellen's "long robe of red velvet" with its fur border, her "arms bare to the elbow" (104), seems sinister. Asking Beaufort to leave, Ellen responds poignantly to Newland's questions about her desire for a divorce, finally saying, with some impatience, "my freedom—is that nothing?" (110).

Newland seems unable to hear. He wants Ellen to deny the accusations in her husband's letter that she has been improperly involved with his secretary. Choosing to assume that no one would believe these charges, Ellen does not answer them. (Wharton's revisions in galley proofs intensify the enigma.)[1] When Newland leaves, having only parroted to Ellen Letterblair's arguments for her dropping the idea of divorce, he is convinced that she is as guilty as the count's letter suggests.

Typical of her expert juxtapositions throughout the novel, Wharton intensifies Newland's discomfort (and calls the reader's attention to his disappointing inarticulateness in the scene with Ellen) by following this scene with that of the lovers' leave-taking in *The Shaughraun,* a scene played without words. Not only does this visualization of Newland-as-lover unable to find words to express his feelings (neither to Ellen or himself) emphasize the real development of the plot, but it also sets up a pattern for subsequent meetings between Ellen and Newland. In many of these interchanges, one or the other pretends not to be aware of the other's presence.

The Age of Innocence often operates through the absence of key characters. In a kind of ellipsis, Wharton chooses to remove protagonists from scenes. She uses this tactic particularly with Ellen, so that our view of her is seldom based on her own actions but instead on either the acts or the reports of others. When Ellen drops out of the text, she becomes an object of someone else's story, and the reader is at the mercy of whomever tells the story. Because the novel is linear and chronological, it seems to be traditional. Yet its chronology follows Newland's actions and so omits much of Ellen's narrative.

Wharton also delights in creating elliptical characterizations. Much of the mystery of both Ellen Olenska and May Welland is that the reader knows so little about who they really are. In some respects, Newland is as responsibile for our knowledge of Ellen as he is for that of May. Wharton makes eminently clear how flawed his view is of the latter, and she suggests that his view of Ellen is likely no more accurate. Her characterizations of the three essential people in the love triangle, then, are skewed to reflect Newland's romantic, self-satisfied perspective. The reader is consequently left with little reliable information about either Ellen or May.

Except for the crucial fact that both are beloved granddaughters of Catherine Mingott ("Catherine the Great"), Ellen and May appear to have little in common. In the eyes of society, perhaps, the women are very different from each other; but one of Wharton's points in the novel is to discredit the monocle of "Society." If one reads *The Age of Innocence* as the story of strong women, beginning with Catherine Spicer Mingott and moving to include both Ellen and May, many of the gaps in the characters of the younger women are filled. By introducing the narrative of Catherine early in the novel, Wharton sets up the paradigm that will provide answers to readers' inquiries.

The daughter of "handsome Bob Spicer" (10), the man who disappeared less than a year after his marriage, absconding with a trust fund and—probably—a beautiful Spanish dancer, Catherine Spicer of Staten Island nevertheless married the wealthy Manson Mingott, who died when she was only 28. She succeeded in freeing his estate for her use, built a remarkable stone house near Central Park, married her daughters abroad, and maintained her remarkably pure reputation: "she had won her way to success by strength of will and hardness of heart, and a kind of haughty effrontery that was somehow justified by the extreme decency and dignity of her private life" (13).

Even more persuasive than Wharton's characterization of Catherine as independent, shrewd, and strong-willed is the fact that she is sometimes wrong. She devalues Ellen's need to be free, aiming to keep her—financially dependent—in the United States, and in her house. The changing social and sexual mores have made at least some of Catherine's values obsolete, and Wharton shows clearly that not even the best-loved young adults can be understood by grandmothers. Conflict between old Catherine and Ellen is inevitable—and it erupts repeatedly. Both women remain strong.

Wharton's various stylistic and narrative devices draw the reader in, and force the reader to help develop the most interesting sets of meanings. From the irony of its title to the acerbity of Catherine's sharp comments about her granddaughters' lives, Wharton's novel seems genuinely part of the modernist movement. Indeed, according to her own essays on fiction, which she began writing for publication in Scribner's magazine soon after completing *The Age of Innocence* (essays collected in 1925 as *The Writing of Fiction*), she had written a modern work.

For Wharton, part of the essence of the modern was the writer's "individualizing"[2] of each character. Dismissing any division between the so-called novel of incident or plot and that of character, she wrote that readers wanted to read about people; what those people did was largely immaterial. Far removed from stereotype, fictional characters were to be "breathing and recognizable human beings" (4). Wharton admired Balzac and Stendhal because of their ability to create such figures; in Balzac's case, Wharton especially liked his women, whom he drew to show their "human contradictions" and how they were "torn with human passions."

Another mark of the modern was that characters existed in real worlds. Wharton's delight in Stendhal's modernity was based on "his insight into the springs of social action" (6). She thought it imperative that lifelike fictional characters grew out of social contexts readers would recognize. (One of Wharton's complaints about some of her contemporaries was that they, in their search for the new, created grotesque or abnormal characters.) According to Wharton, both Balzac and Stendhal wrote about people who might have existed—but they also viewed "each character first of all as a product of particular material or social conditions" (6–7). She goes on to explain that "Drama, situation, is made out of the conflicts thus produced between social order and individual appetites" (13–14).

Wharton's belief in the importance of the relationship between character and social context explains part of the power of *The Age of Innocence*. Newland Archer cannot be dissociated from his culture any more than May Welland can stand separate from that same milieu. So deftly, and economically, does Wharton mesh character and society that the book illustrates her own insistent principle that the chief mark of a good writer is the ability to select. The best writer finds "crucial moments from the welter of existence" (14)—or "illuminating" incidents (109)—and uses them to focus the reader's attention. Through these moments, characterization becomes clear: plot, motivation, and explicit character analysis fuse to form "a shaft driven straight into the heart of human experience" (36).

The Writing of Fiction is filled with specific comments about point of view, according to Wharton the writer's most difficult problem (87); the sparing use of dialogue (72); and the choice of the right beginning (100). It also approaches the larger questions of form in the novel. Rather than use the notion of organic form then current among modernists, Wharton puts forth that the length of the work must be determined by the "lapse of time" needed to show the changes in characters' "successive states of feeling" (72). For example, Wharton praises Jane Austen for her "impeccable" sense of proportion (106).

In its emphasis on the way the writer achieves mastery, Wharton's book initiates a modernist discourse about technique. Relevant to both the oeuvre of modernism and to Wharton's own work, her primer about writing fiction complements the novels she wrote in postwar years. Of these, *The Age of Innocence* works as succinctly, and as subtly, as any 1920s novel by writers usually categorized as modern. Less cynical than F. Scott Fitzgerald's *The Great Gatsby* (1925) and less fragmented than Ernest Hemingway's *The Sun Also Rises* (1926), *The Age of Innocence* similarly interrogates cultural beliefs about romantic love, respectability, success, and class. And Wharton's novel, using these incipient modernist strategies, asks these questions first.

8

The Age of Innocence as Newland Archer's Novel

Wharton's 1920 novel is ultimately modern in that it continually frustrates readers' expectations. Moreover, it somewhat ironically tweaks these expectations, leaving clues for the observant reader as to the apparent direction of the story, but then taking the narrative in a different direction. Even though Newland does not run away with Ellen early in his life, for example, the last chapter—with May's death freeing him from his earlier vows—promises reunion. But, true to Wharton's cagey narrative method, no reunion occurs.

Unexpected and troubling as it is, the ending of *The Age of Innocence* throws the reader back into a serious consideration of the character of the male protagonist. Newland Archer most assuredly has it in his power to meet Ellen, and to woo her. For him to refuse even the first act makes the reader question the character Wharton has initially drawn. The first thread in the book's fabric of carefully crafted ironies comes to be that "Newland Archer," a man named for strength and poise, combined with the suggestion of unexplored and fertile territory, does not live up to his name. Who is this character with the winning name who seems not to be a hero?

In many scenes, in fact, Newland appears more foolish than heroic. There are his several attempts to avoid seeing Ellen by playing some wishful child's game: if she turns around, I will go to her. As an adult who is supposedly in love with this woman, willfully giving up opportunities to be with her appears foolhardy. Similarly, Newland's frantic search at the Blenkers' home, when he is propelled by the sight of what he believes is Ellen's pink parasol, serves no purpose except to ridicule his overly romantic attitudes.

Finding the parasol as he looks for Ellen, he is in the midst of kissing its handle when Wharton provides one of her deceptive paragraphs:

> He heard a rustle of skirts against the box, and sat motionless, leaning on the parasol handle with clapsed hands, and letting the rustle come nearer without lifting his eyes. He had always known that this must happen . . . "Oh, Mr. Archer!" exclaimed a loud young voice. (226)

Voice, like parasol, belonging to the youngest Blenker daughter, Newland is shaken from his romantic dream to learn that Ellen has been called to Boston. As Miss Blenker chatters, the broken-hearted Archer continues his self-pitying internal monologue:

> His whole future seemed suddenly to be unrolled before him, and passing down its endless emptiness he saw the dwindling figure of a man to whom nothing was ever to happen. (227)

Taking action, Newland finds Ellen in Boston and asks her to spend the day with him on a steamboat. After being married for 18 months, he finally can no longer resist what he thinks is the ruling passion of his life.

During that day, the level of Newland's self-delusion does not change. He courts Ellen, protests his love, and laments his unhappiness—a discourse hardly calculated to impress the worldly countess with its reasonableness. She honors its passion, however, and they talk of their mutual sacrifice:

"What's the use?" [Archer asks.] "You gave me my first glimpse of
a real life, and at the same moment you asked me to go with a
sham one. It's beyond human enduring—that's all."
        "Oh, don't say that; when I'm enduring it!" she burst out,
her eyes filling. (243)

Enduring his marriage and his life becomes Newland's focus during his second year as May's husband, but his passion for Ellen continues to obscure his vision.

That he cannot know himself in the extremity of his grief over
the loss of Ellen is clear when he looks at May, in Wharton's words,
"with the startled gaze of a stranger" (189). A man who claims to value
honesty above all other traits, Newland sees that he is caught in a
relentless web of lies as he plays the role of loving husband even while
distraught with his passion for Ellen. Lying to May about the reason
for his trips away is only the tip of the iceberg. More frightening are
his reflections to himself as he watches his wife: "'How young she is!
For what endless years this life will have to go on!'" (266). In a later
scene, when Newland opens a window against his wife's protests, he
vents his frustration in silently wishing May dead:

> The sensation of standing there, in that warm familiar room, and
> looking at her, and wishing her dead, was so strange, so fascinat-
> ing and overmastering, that its enormity did not immediately
> strike him. He simply felt that chance had given him a new possi-
> bility to which his sick soul might cling. Yes, May might die—peo-
> ple did: young people, healthy people like herself: she might die,
> and set him suddenly free. (296)

Wharton gives the reader the right word—"enormity"—but then
continues to show Newland's stubborn retreat from the reality of his
situation.

After Catherine Mingott calls for Ellen following her stroke,
Newland has two hours alone with his beloved in the brougham en
route to her grandmother's. When he tells her that he trusts that his
vision of the two of them united will come true, Ellen corrects him:

"'we'll look, not at visions, but at realities'" (289) and then asks if she is to live with Newland as his "mistress." Choosing the crudest language possible, Ellen hopes to cut through Newland's illusions. His answer, however, is still utter romantic nonsense:

> "I want—I want somehow to get away with you into a world where words like that—categories like that—won't exist. Where we shall be simply two human beings who love each other, who are the whole of life to each other; and nothing else on earth will matter." She drew a deep sigh that ended in another laugh. "Oh, my dear—where is that country? Have you ever been there?" (290)

The point of Wharton's dialogue here, as in many scenes between Ellen and Newland, is that the woman's language is much less romantic than the man's. Anticipated social roles have been exchanged, social attitudes reversed. The result of Newland's expressing such unrealistic sentiments (even if the reader sympathizes with him) is that the relationships between Newland and both May and Ellen start to become clear.

The key to understanding Archer's character is to see the narrative in terms of its "time elapsed." Wharton structures the book as she does because the reader must understand that Archer's infatuation with Ellen Olenska does not diminish over time. It rather grows into obsession. His marriage to May is, accordingly, at greater risk months after the ceremony than initially. Wharton puts forth in *The Writing of Fiction* that the purpose of writing a novel rather than a story or a novella is to allow for the development of character (*Writing*, 76); having said that, she uses the sometimes tortuous and long path of *The Age of Innocence* ironically. Newland Archer's character does not, strictly speaking, ever develop. Caught in the romantic world of the adolescent imagination, he instead beats his stubborn will against the impenetrable walls of family tradition, social custom, ritualized love, and human values. Although Ellen understands his passion, or what he defines as passion, she cannot bear to watch his behavior—and so she is often absent.

The Age of Innocence *as Newland Archer's Novel*

What Wharton achieves in *The Age of Innocence* is a circular narrative. The reader cannot decipher the reasons for Newland's acts in the beginning of the work until almost the end of the story. It goes against all expected fictional practice that the author has written a book about a less-than-heroic figure. The reader, consequently, keeps looking for Newland's nobility, his heroism; based on the book's plot, that quality seems to be equated with his overpowering love for Ellen. Yet Wharton has constructed the book so that eventually the reader comes to see that the ostensible narrative has become something other: the story of Newland Archer's great passion has segued into the story of the culture Newland Archer represents, complete with all its stolidity, judgmental thinking, and sham.

The mixture of elements such a focus requires poses a difficult problem for the novelist. How to begin with a scene that shows that entire society? In one way, by opening *The Age of Innocence* at the opera, Wharton accomplishes this view of society. But the reader is largely unaware of the wide-angle lens, because Wharton's attention seems to fall chiefly on Newland. In this first chapter, she shows him trying to play a heroic role—going to his fiancée and her family to help counter the ugly gossip that could harm the entire group, offering up the announcement of his and May's engagement to mute the talk about the Countess Olenska. As Wharton notes in *The Writing of Fiction*, "The question where to begin" is crucial for the novelist; "the art of seizing on the right moment" becomes key to the entire book (*Writing*, 100).

More to the point when one considers the effect of the novel as a whole, the author continues, "no conclusion can be right which is not latent in the first page" (*Writing*, 108). Her strategy in giving Newland the spotlight, then, both in the early scenes of the book and throughout, allows her to devote that enigmatic last chapter to what readers have considered his puzzling refusal to even visit Ellen. Wharton's words, the structure of a novel must be shaped by "inevitability" (*Writing*, 108). By finding Newland's behavior surprising, readers have admitted that they have read *The Age of Innocence* as a romance or a marriage novel—rather than as a novel of character, or of characters caught in a seamless tapestry of social coercion. For

Wharton, the intentional, consummate novelist, Newland Archer's failure at the end of the book is as predictable, and as inevitable, as his somewhat pompous "rescue" of the Mingott family at its beginning.

The mark of the greatness of Wharton's art, however, is that her novel succeeds in making all its central characters not only understandable, but sympathetic. Deflating the character of Newland Archer is not a primary aim of *The Age of Innocence*. Rather, showing his own romantic innocence becomes one of Wharton's strategies for creating sympathy for him. All the world loves a lover, and Newland's continuing to play that unfulfilled role keeps him seeming to be a positive figure.

Ironically, he continues to be positive despite the fact that in nearly every scene, Wharton makes him foolish. It is this subversive undercutting of the traditional role of hero that leads to the reader's eventual recognition of what *The Age of Innocence* means. Here, Wharton says in *The Writing of Fiction*, the subject of the work is less important than what the novelist finds in that subject, and to what moral judgment it might lead. Hoping for a "vital radiation" from the reader's immersion in the text, the author chooses as subject a narrative that "must contain in itself something that sheds a light on our moral experience" (*Writing*, 26).

In a chaos-driven society such as the postwar years created, with women's freedoms given rhetoric but no real efficacy, Wharton saw that marriage as a cultural institution was even more significant than it had been during the 19th century. Marriage protected women; it insured them—and their children—financial support as well as respectability. Although the tradition of the romance novel might create sympathy for men caught in the shackles of that institution (a typically romantic stance toward monogamy, the observant Wharton probably noted), in real life men needed that link to responsibility. Otherwise, like balloons without weights, they airily flew from woman to woman. Such utter lack of responsibility, social philosophers might have said, was a blot on any human social system.

Setting *The Age of Innocence* 50 years earlier protected the aging Wharton from charges of old-fogyism; it also used her keen memories of the time to marvelous effect. And it gave her a way to criticize sharply the rootless, manipulative relationships she saw around her and heard of in her countless letters from women friends both in the

United States and abroad. Men needed to be reminded of their responsibilities to the fairer sex—fairer and, usually, less powerful and less financially able. As if Wharton hadn't herself learned the lessons of the foibles of men's passions, not only watching her husband Teddy fall in love with other (and younger) women, but being subjected to seeing the same kinds of behavior from both Morton Fullerton and Walter Berry, she was bombarded with examples from friends after World War I ended. She wrote years later to a younger friend, "Why do the young still marry? . . . I suppose it's a case of a purely obsolete and fetishistic act being performed automatically by a generation which has completely forgotten what it meant."[1]

Wharton was too good a writer to expound a moral message in anything she wrote. She does say, somewhat wryly, in *The Writing of Fiction,* "True originality consists not in a new manner but in a new vision. That new, that personal, vision is attained only by looking long enough at the object respresented to make it the writer's own . . ." (*Writing,* 18). If Wharton's subject, six years after her divorce from Teddy and (perhaps) several years after the peak of her intimacy with Walter Berry, is the cavalier attitude American men had toward the institution of marriage, no reader should be surprised. What is surprising is that this seemingly nostalgic look at New York culture during the 1870s has so personal a subtext.

It seems clear that what was new about the author's look at that culture was the kind of vision she presents. Her response is very far from nostalgia, or valorization of romantic passion, or overriding sympathy for the artistic Newland as he is caught in the confines of what he calls a deadening marriage to May. The complexity of not only her subject, but of her attitudes toward it, made writing *The Age of Innocence* one of Wharton's most difficult writing tasks.

Much of the vitality of the novel, for readers in the 1990s as well as those contemporary with the work, comes from the fact that Newland Archer remains reasonably complex. Although critic Grace Kellogg dismissed him by explaining the ending as a typical "retreat" for Archer (based on her reading of "his retreat from every crisis"[2]), Cynthia Griffin Wolff reads the novel as Archer's bildungsroman, saying that in it Wharton "traces Archer's struggle to mature, to become in some continuous and authentic way—himself. She lays before us the present and the possible in such a way that the middle-aged man who concludes the novel seems an admirable and significant outgrowth of the untried youth at the beginning."[3] Whatever sympathy the reader has for Newland, then, comes from that fact that he has so few choices—because of his innate respect for his social system. According to Wolff, Newland's search is "entirely internal. He cannot flee the provincial world of old New York; he must learn to transmute it into something valuable."[4] What that something is reflects Wharton's own lessons from a disappointing romantic life: "acceptance of reality and dedication to generativity."[5]

Wolff uses Ellen Olenska's tribute to Newland's moral stand as a means of confirming how positive his choices finally are, although she admits that at the time Ellen praises him, he does not yet see these traits in himself. "Ellen has taken empty words and imputed significance to them, yet hers is not an act of such wistful longing as we might suppose. She may love a man who does not yet fully exist, but she has fixed her affections on what is potential and possible in Newland; and if he is not yet the man she judges him to be, there are clear indications that he has already committed himself to becoming that man."[6]

With all the artistry she possessed, Wharton drew the fragile Archer so that he maintains reader sympathy even as he disappoints the reader's interest in romantic fulfillment. With an irony that would not have been lost on Wharton, she did so by making him the love object of the character who is the true heart of the novel, Ellen Olenska.

9

The Age of Innocence as Ellen Olenska's Novel

The Age of Innocence is more complex than some moral fable, and it is the interrelationships among the three leading characters that prove Wharton's narrative expertise. Even though readers are trained to read a text with special attention to male characters, in this novel, Ellen Olenska and May Welland almost irresistibly become centers of interest. (In such earlier fiction as "Bunner Sisters," *The Touchstone, The Valley of Decision, Ethan Frome,* and *The Reef,* Wharton creates two women characters who share qualities, and dilemmas, that make them parts of a whole. In her use of a kind of "double heroine," she may have been searching for satisfying ways women could respond to social pressures and mandates that otherwise seemed impossible to satisfy.)

As we have seen, some critics have suggested that Wharton was herself enacting the role of Newland Archer, that she was somehow—with all her brilliant success as a serious writer—more like a man than a woman. What might be more helpful for any reader of *The Age of Innocence* is the sense that Wharton as author was in some way sympathetic to, and capable of identifying with, all three of her lead characters.

In May Welland, Wharton could reexperience her own role as debutante, the daughter of a prominent family, poised to be a "catch" for some eligible young man very early in her career. (Wharton was writing fiction and poetry even before her debut at 17. In a way, her mother's rushing her into society was a way of "correcting" her ambition to be a writer, an ambition her social set wanted neither to understand nor sanction.) Just as Wharton endured an unsatisfactory marriage for 25 years, ignoring infidelities and various misuses of her personal funds, May was trying to live that proper life, free of scandal, intent on being a good wife and a respected member of her social set.

If May Welland is the nascent Wharton, Ellen Olenska is the achieved and successful adult woman. Above all, she is the woman who has come to love France, the country that allowed her the freedom to be herself, the country that respected intellect and valued privacy. In France, one could exist as a self, an identity, a person— regardless of the way that person meshed, or perhaps failed to mesh, with society. If America was dominated by the prerogatives of social class or the mandates of what good citizenship in a community entailed, France was more likely to be a loose collection of free spirits, each intent on actualization in some separate sphere of individuality.

So Wharton's being removed from America, much as she might miss some elements of that life, was less a tragedy than it was an opportunity for personal fulfillment. Consequently, in her notebooks, when Wharton planned to have Ellen marry Newland and live that "old New York" life, she suddenly realized what such a life would mean: frustration, boredom, the loss of both fruitful peace and tantalizing excitement.

By the time she wrote *The Age of Innocence*, Wharton also had experienced enough sexual passion that she could write more completely about human beings in love. The restraint (and sometimes outright disguise) that marked her treatment of love in such an early work as *The House of Mirth* here gives way to the genuine physical frustration of being unable to touch, or even to be near, the beloved. The presence of Ellen Olenska radiates through the novel, so that for all its limitation in point of view, Newland Archer's love is validated whenever she is in sight. Wharton is in this way like her creation of Ellen. Like Ellen, she has known passion. And also like Ellen, she is capable of living alone and being independent. The thought of loneliness does not frighten her. If Ellen lives without Archer, she at least holds the memory of their shared love in trust.

Although May and Ellen are cousins, and Wharton suggests that Ellen is not much older than May, the difference in their life experience is immense. Ellen Olenska becomes, in a way, the completion of May Welland. A woman midway through the life pattern, a woman who has made the Cinderella-type choices (married to a count, she presumably expected to live happily ever after), Ellen is now faced with that dominant theme of modern letters—for women characters as well as for men—self-actualization, self-fulfillment, and, in the subtext of this novel, sexual fulfillment, a topic so "modern" Wharton cannot even breathe it.

The similarities between Wharton and Newland Archer involve their love of reading and philosophy. Self-educated through foreign travel, tutors, language instruction—the best of the literate and artistic world—Wharton was proud of her knowledge and her taste. She did not, for example, hobnob in Paris with the avant-garde or such young expatriates as Ernest Hemingway; she kept to her own circles even in the excitement of modernism. Wharton lived a formal, high-class life, and she did not give up the privileges of that class easily.

She was also an idealist. Many of Newland's soliloquies voice thoughts that Wharton expressed in letters to friends. In some ways, Newland's monologues can also be given to Ellen—the sharply restricted narrative point of view makes investigation of her interior life impossible. The would-be lovers are alike in many ways. Just as they love books and art, they also create fantasies about the freedoms, and fulfillments, of travel. Yet of the two, Ellen is the person who travels (think how many places she lives just in the months of the novel), as if her physical movement reflects that of her eager intelligence. No one else in the book has so many changes of address.

And no one else so hungers for experience. Intent on draining life to the lees, despite what danger may rest there, Ellen in this configuration suggests her author, Edith Wharton, as well as the character from Russian fiction that Wharton so admired—Anna Karenina.[1] As women who dared to lead their own lives, Ellen, Anna, and Wharton understood what being outside social boundaries meant. Occasionally they yearned to return to confinement, but more often they felt ful-filled in their independent quests.

Wharton portrays Ellen Olenska in *The Age of Innocence* as an apparently thoroughly confident woman, moving through life with a refreshing lack of self-consciousness. She comes to the opera box eager to be reacquainted with childhood friends; as grateful as she is for peo-ple's kindnesses, she is not self-deprecating. There is even some humor in her discourse, suggesting that she does not take herself (or her soci-ety) too seriously.

She is also willing to risk her place in that society, if it should conflict with what she sees as important duties. Struggling to secure a divorce, going out when and where she is invited, and braving society's opinion to visit Regina Dallas after Beaufort's failure, the Countess Olenska takes New York in stride. Her firm sense of self is not disori-ented with geographic change.

In the modern age, when women's recognition of their sexuality had become one of the chief marks of achieved, mature womanhood, Ellen Olenska's relinquishment of sexual satisfaction becomes even more heroic. Whether or not we understand why Ellen loves Newland as much as she seems to, Wharton wants us to believe that her love for him is the grand passion of her life. Her giving him up, then, so that May's child can have its rightful father, is heroic.

As we have seen, Wharton works hard to make Newland worth the sacrifice. In one of the most moving scenes between them, Ellen tells him that she stays in the United States because of him: "it was you who made me understand that under the dullness there are things so fine and sensitive and delicate that even those I most cared for in my other life look cheap in comparison . . . it seems as if I'd never before understood with how much that is hard and shabby and base the most exquisite pleasures may be paid" (241). When Newland emotionally confronts her with the unhappiness of his marriage, and therefore of his life, she coun-ters wisely, "If it's not worth while to have given up, to have missed things, so that others may be saved from disillusionment and misery— then everything I came home for, everything that made my other life seem by contrast so bare and so poor because no one there took account of them—all these things are a sham or a dream—" (242).

The Age of Innocence *as Ellen Olenska's Novel*

It is in this scene, too, that Ellen insists on being "perfectly honest" with Newland (241), a phrase that recalls Wharton's childhood aim to make herself "a rigid rule of absolute, unmitigated truth-telling" (*LI*, 1073). Through such relentless honesty, the child Edith was to reach those superior ethical heavens where her own unorthodoxies could not mar her integrity. She writes with poignance of her "first sense of moral bewilderment—of the seeming impossibility of reconciling an ideal of conduct with the unexpectedness of human experience" (*LI*, 1073–74). Wharton learned young that abstract belief could all too quickly shift ground, particularly when one was faced with real people caught in real conflicts.

If May is Diana the huntress, the boyish and androgynous "new" woman, ready to preserve her hearth by any means (including tearing to bits people who threaten that hearth), then Ellen is a softer, older, and wiser woman, a mortal woman rather than a goddess. She needs an avenger for her own innocence, because she will not act or speak for herself. She lets Newland believe that she has lived with her husband's secretary, even though Wharton's later introduction of M. Rivière as an educated, personable, and clearly moral man answers the count's accusations. Responding to the count's charges is something Ellen will not deign to do—and Newland is so naive that he takes her silence as an admission of guilt.

Like this piece of information, there are many other segments of Ellen Olenska's story missing. The gaps in her narrative, however, do more than handicap the reader in charting her growth to the enviable maturity she has reached by the time of the novel's action. Wharton's intentional gaps force the reader to imagine those episodes that might have led to Ellen's maturity. Some scenes between the young American bride and her European husband would have been sexually based; others would have had to do with what Wharton considered the primary human qualities of honesty and integrity, and these are even more difficult for the reader to reconstruct.

Wharton suggests some of the ingredients of Ellen's childhood in the passages describing her later philosophical acceptance of the macabre life (and romances) of her guardian aunt, Medora Manson. Introduced in the novel as the companion of the founder of the cult of love, Dr. Agathon Carver, Medora clearly wants her niece to reconcile with "poor Stanislas." As she tells Newland about Ellen's life with the count, she embroiders the lush court atmosphere and pictures the countess receiving "the homage of the greatest."

> . . . on the material side, Mr. Archer, if one may stoop to consider such things; do you know what she is giving up? Those roses there on the sofa—acres like them, under glass and in the open, in his matchless terraced gardens at Nice! Jewels—historic pearls: the Sobieski emeralds—sables—but she cares nothing for all those! Art and beauty, those she does care for, she lives for, as I always have; and those also surround her. Pictures, priceless furniture, music, brilliant conversation—ah, that, my dear young man, if you'll excuse me, is what you've no conception of here. . . . (160–61)

Medora chatters on, flicking her "absurd ivory fan," unable to see how horrified Newland is at the thought of Ellen's returning to her spouse.

Rather than being annoyed with her foolish aunt, Ellen is compassionate and kind. She worries about Medora's infatuation with Dr. Carver, and about her willingness to be a pawn for Olenski. Although the two women are worlds apart in taste and morality, Ellen defers to her guardian so long as she can do so without compromising her own integrity. Later in the novel, she lives with Medora, sharing what little income she has with her impoverished relative.

Ellen behaves similarly toward her grandmother, her Aunt Welland, and May. Always gracious and perspicacious, she appears thankful for her relatives' efforts to help her live in the American culture. But her gratitude never shakes her independence; she never relinquishes control of her own decision-making.

Ellen's openness to others, even as she maintains her own strong core of independence, suggests a fluidity of personality that makes her a bit chameleonlike. But as Wharton notes in *The Writing of Fiction,* the creation of realistic characters depends on the author's being "continuously aware that the bounds of personality are not reproducible by a sharp black line, but that each of us flows imperceptibly into adjacent people and things" (7). In some respects, the writer, too, partakes of these permeable borders. Ideally, Wharton contends, the novelist "has so let his subject ripen in his mind that the characters are as close to him as his own flesh. To the novelist who lives among his creations in this continuous intimacy they should pour out their tale" (88). It seems likely that Ellen Olenska was of more than casual interest to the author at this period of her own life, as she was assessing her existence as one of stabilizing, aging, and—in some ways—renouncing.

Perhaps the most important quality of Ellen Olenska as Wharton created her for *The Age of Innocence* is that she remains alive. Given the evocative but pathetic suicide of Lily Bart in *The House of Mirth*, the fact that Wharton had clearly determined that Ellen Olenska was going to live is crucial. Ellen is also no ingenue. A married woman, a woman with sexual experience and knowledge of the demimonde, a woman who has her own income (or would, if she returned to her husband)—little Ellen Mingott is hardly the naïf that New York society likes to think she is. Nor is she the "dark lady, pale and dark, who would look up quickly, half rise, and hold out a long thin hand with three rings on it" (361) of Newland's faltering imagination. She is, rather, the enigmatic but powerful center of Wharton's most suggestive, and most sensual, novel.

10

The Age of Innocence as May Welland's Story

Evelyn Bracasso is one of the few critics who has found May Welland a positive character. Praising May's "toughness and tenacity, the depth of feeling and strength of character" (*Writing,* 135), this critic describes the way Wharton's use of May's eyes throughout *The Age of Innocence* reveals her true comprehension of the undercurrents of Newland's behavior.

What Bracasso does not mention is that May is a more subtle rendering of the woman intent on marriage: Wharton's best-known portrait of that lady was, of course, Undine Spragg of *The Custom of the Country,* the novel (except for her war writings and *Summer*) closest in time of composition to this one. While May is cast much more sympathetically than Undine, both are young women fully aware of what a "good" marriage is, and what such a marriage can do for their—and their families'—futures. Undine pretends to be more virginal than she is, while the reader has no reason to question May's virginity. But in Wharton's characterization of both women, their natures are drawn to be more manipulative than passionate. More to the point, neither May nor Undine interested Wharton in themselves; they are necessary for her exploration of women's roles in—and out of—marriage.

The Age of Innocence *as May Welland's Story*

There was no way Wharton could avoid writing about marriage, and about the thousands of women who planned their lives toward that end. The Victorian Age had created the True Woman, the sexually naive and pure helpmeet whose sole purpose was to be wife and mother to husband and children. Inscribed by religious, economic, and social codes, the role of True Woman reinforced patriarchal power in all spheres of society. Being a True Woman was less arduous than having to make a living independently, of course, and a good many women—unless they were Kate Chopin's Edna Pontellier—found such duty far from unpleasant. Marriage was woman's accepted, and desired, future. (In *The Age of Innocence*, Wharton does not even attempt to portray a working woman, as she had in the character of Gerty Farish in *The House of Mirth*.) In the 1870s elite New York culture, everyone married. The significant social choice was whether or not to stay that way.

In this novel, Wharton uses the Welland family relationships to illustrate the classic patriarchal unit. Funded by Mr. Welland, the family is actually run—and organized to the specific detail—by his powerful wife. The family seemingly operates for his comfort: so that he does not take a winter chill, the entire household moves to Florida each spring. Wharton's wry tone suggests her view of such togetherness:

> Mr. Welland was a mild and silent man, with no opinions but with many habits. With these habits none might interfere; and one of them demanded that his wife and daughter should always go with him on his annual journey to the south. To preserve an unbroken domesticity was essential to his peace of mind; he would not have known where his hair-brushes were or how to provide stamps for his letters, if Mrs. Welland had not been there to tell him. As all the members of the family adored each other, and as Mr. Welland was the central object of their idolatry, it never occurred to his wife and May to let him go to St. Augustine alone. . . . (118)

Because Wharton avoids any intimate look at the Wellands, she leaves her reader little choice but to accept them as being as superficial as her description suggests.

In *The Age of Innocence,* Wharton also creates a larger-than-usual share of unmarried women, such as Newland's sister, the over-protected Janey Archer, whose passion for untoward gossip grows strangely out of her sheltered life; and of women alone—whether they are no longer married because of death or divorce. Catherine Mingott, Medora Manson, and Mrs. Archer herself comprise a veritable gallery of women, all perfectly capable of making it on their own, given enough income and social position. (The fragility of Medora Manson's situation stems from the fact that she has so little money.) These characters provide the reader with information about the choices Ellen Olenska faces: without a husband, and without income, one is prey to whomever can provide money.

If in *The Custom of the Country* Wharton unleashes her scarcely disguised contempt for women who plan their lives purposely to marry, and only toward that end, by the time of *The Age of Innocence,* she views such women as products of their culture. More sympathetic to May than to Undine, Wharton uses her point-of-view narrator to underscore how smart the Welland daughter is. By using Newland's perceptions of May, which the reader understands immediately are too simplified to be accurate, Wharton portrays May to show how mistaken Newland is about his fiancée. The truth is that May does not need his education: she has been educated in a full panoply of wiles and strategies. She is a veteran in her mother's, and her society's, preparation for courtship, engagement, and marriage.

May is the True Woman, junior version. She is virginal. She is dedicated to the life of self-sacrifice for her husband and children. She is also "the American girl," the frank and honest person who, according to Wharton, "had nothing to conceal" (45). When Newland chooses her to become Mrs. Archer, he is not entirely wrong in his choice. This is Wharton's description of the May Welland Newland knows:

> He delighted in the radiant good looks of his betrothed, in her health, her horsemanship, her grace and quickness at games, and the shy interest in books and ideas that she was beginning to develop under his guidance. . . . She was straight-forward, loyal

and brave; she had a sense of humour (chiefly proved by her laughing at his jokes); and he suspected, in the depths of her inno-cently-gazing soul, a glow of feeling that it would be a joy to waken. (45)

Positive qualities all, but Wharton takes care to mention that even early in their courtship, Newland feels oppressed by "this creation of factitious purity." He wonders where, and who, the real May is.

Archer admires May's health and athletic abilities; she has never pretended to be the protected Victorian woman. She is a successful sportswoman, as her winning the archery contest shows. Lest the reader miss the full significance of May's athletic abilities, Wharton describes the contest itself and then extends this incident by moving to the post-victory scene at Catherine Mingott's. Here May's grand-mother congratulates her, admires the diamond-tipped arrow brooch that is her prize, and jokes with her about the need to leave so valuable a memento to her own daughter. May's blush at the thought of having children, after more than a year of marriage, emphasizes the feigned innocence her culture demands.

The visit itself recalls the early betrothal visit, when Catherine both compliments May on the engagement ring and suggests that Newland have May's hands modeled while they are abroad. She notes somewhat sadly that May's hands are large—"'it's these modern sports that spread the joints'"—but she finds solace in the fact that, no matter how modern her granddaughter is, the skin of her hands remains white (29).

The earlier scene ironically suggests that Newland is in control of everything. A suitable representative of the patriarchy, he has chosen a proper (even luxurious) ring, a large sapphire, its new setting signify-ing his avant-garde tendencies. The family heirloom is appropriate, as is his having something distinctively his own added to the ring. But by the time of the archery scene, the tenor of the visit changes: now May's prize is the icon of the arrow, bejeweled at its tip with a dia-mond, the hardest substance possible and also the most valuable. Newland and May have, of course, married; and Newland Archer has shared his name with his wife. Now also an Archer, May has become fully empowered. It is one of Wharton's beautifully structured ironies that Newland, from this point on in the narrative, does not know what is going on. He also seems unaware that his wife is not only talented at archery, but that she also is (at least figuratively) well armed.

Wharton structures both the couple's visits to Catherine so that Ellen Olenska is in the household at the time. During the betrothal visit, the countess appears late in the visit, escorted unfortunately by Julius Beaufort. During the archery contest visit, Ellen does not appear. Instead, Catherine sends Newland to find and fetch her, and it is at this moment that Wharton shows Newland's tendency to fantasize and rationalize, to contrive to miss seeing Ellen. The two visits, seemingly so much alike, actually mark the clear change in Newland's attitude toward his passion for Ellen. Now clandestine even in his acceptance of his love for her, he avoids any contact with the woman he believes is his great love. Newland has become content with his imaginary life; indeed, he prefers to live apart from the reality of his marriage to May, and any possible involvement with Ellen.

As has been suggested, May is similar in many ways to Ellen. She is a younger, yet still mirroring, version of her cosmopolitan cousin. Both women are beautiful (though Beaufort prefers Ellen's appeal). Both are from excellent families. Both are prizes in the marriage market that runs society in New York and the other capitals of the world. Both are women of some charm, and, so far as the reader knows, of integrity, honor, and sexual reticence. To the reader, however, whose knowledge of both women comes largely through Newland's eyes, May Welland and the Countess Olenska would seem to be creatures from different planets.

What is finally most significant about the women's relationship throughout *The Age of Innocence* is the way Wharton uses it to show how the Mingott-Welland family (May included) is observing, and judging, Ellen's friendship with Newland. At first, Ellen's relatives are protective of her. Rallying around when society refuses to attend the Lovell Mingotts' dinner in her honor, the Wellands and the Archers create the van der Luyden occasion as an alternative.

Shortly after Newland has been to tea at Ellen's, and has sent yellow roses without his card, the atmosphere begins to change. Uneasy about Ellen's socializing with Beaufort, Mrs. Struthers, and the artistic crowd, the family also sees what an expense keeping Ellen's household might become. Their move to convince her to return to her husband, achieved—ironically—through Newland's advice, is financially rather than emotionally motivated. They do not dislike Ellen, but they are not convinced she is worth the trouble she is causing. Ellen Olenska is so very visible.

When Newland travels to Florida (to avoid another tête-à-tête with Ellen but apparently to urge May to set their wedding date during the spring), May's interrogation of him is purposely misleading. Wharton signals the reader by saying that May's look "suddenly . . . changed and deepened inscrutably" (146). Suggesting that Newland is still involved with his mistress saves May from confronting him about his feelings for Ellen. Later, by agreeing to be married in a month, May cuts short the progress of Newland and Ellen's love.

The author's handling of May and Newland's wedding has been mentioned as an example of Wharton's structural finesse. While Newland exists in his fantasy world, imagining that he sees the absent Ellen Olenska at every turn, the ceremony joins him with May. And as his bride says when they drive away from the church, nothing bad will ever happen now, "as long as we two are together" (187).

Months after the wedding, Newland begins to realize that while May and other members of the family have news of Ellen, he does not. He also becomes aware that May's feelings toward her cousin have grown hostile. On one occasion May says that Ellen is so "'changed . . . . So indifferent to her friends, I mean. . . . I sometimes think we've always bored her.'" The stunned Newland remains quiet, "and she continued, with a tinge of hardness that he had never before noticed in her frank fresh voice: 'After all, I wonder if she wouldn't be happier with her husband'" (217).

Here, and frequently throughout the rest of the novel, May casts Ellen in the role of fickle woman, changeable and changing, with the implication that she has abandoned the values New York believes are important (i.e., she has lived too long abroad). The fault, then, is with Ellen—her strange behavior, her inexplicably refusing large sums of money from the count, but more important, refusing to return to him

as his wife. Given that Ellen has changed, and that her family is frus-
trated with her, May is no longer honor-bound to be honest with her
(or with Newland).

Into this patterning of a gradual disaffiliation between Ellen and
her family, Newland's impassioned meetings with the countess seem
even more ill-timed. His relentless pursuit of her is more evidence of
his own alienation from both his marriage and his real surroundings.
May's desperate lie to Ellen about her supposed pregnancy is her final
attempt to try to stop the flood tide of emotion that she can see rising
in Newland's consciousness. That it works, calling from Ellen the kind
of compassion and justness that she knows is the proper response,
lessens the guilt May feels for her duplicity.

Wharton's scene-setting for May's announcement to Newland is
once again masterful. Wearing her remodeled wedding gown to the
opera, May hopes to evoke memories of their pristine love. Near the
breaking point, Newland asks May to leave the performance of *Faust*
(a replica of that with which the novel, and Newland's love for Ellen,
begins). May falls as she steps out of the carriage, muddying and tearing her dress. Using the damaged gown as a metaphor for the ruined
marrriage, Wharton prepares the reader for Newland's confession of
his passion for Ellen.

May, however, forestalls his words. Looking at him with conveniently "transparent eyes," May tells him "with her unshaken can-
dour" (which, the reader has come to understand, is not candor at all,
but rather May's version of whatever truth she thinks Newland can
bear) that Ellen is leaving the country (324). It is not until the end of
the following chapter that Newland (and the reader) is apprised of
May's falsehood. By telling Ellen that she is pregnant, May has stifled
her hope of ever loving Newland. And as May tells her husband about
their child, after their dinner in honor of Ellen's departure several
weeks later, Wharton describes succinctly the triumphant May, her
eyes "wet with victory" (343).

May's machinations continue. Trapped into domesticity with the
eventual responsibilities of a wife and three children, Newland never
gets to Paris—nor does he ever see Ellen. But his son Dallas has it
wrong at the end, when he seems to praise the fact that his mother and

father never talked to each other about anything. Newland takes this comment as a compliment; in Wharton's lexicon, it is not. Wharton would not have sanctioned a husband-wife relationship in which neither party is honest with the other. Dallas, too, will learn that silences in intimacy are even more destructive than the silences elsewhere in society.

The ending of *The Age of Innocence* is, then, not intended to valorize May and Newland's marriage. That Newland falls into May's last trap is, for Wharton, a sorrow. For finally, the nostalgic memory of his wife's knowing what was in his mind and heart all those years keeps him—even after May's death—away from Ellen. May has been more victorious than even she could have hoped.

11

Daughters and Mothers, Wharton's Pervasive Theme

Wharton's reluctance to delve into relationships between mothers and daughters has usually been ascribed to her relationship with her own mother. Because she mistrusted her mother, she found even imagining a good rapport with children difficult. Her investigation of the mother-daughter bond in *The Age of Innocence* has more in common with her early configurations of the relationship than with her later ones, such as those in the novels *The Mother's Recompense* and *Twilight Sleep*, when she finally stops faulting the mother figure.

In *The Age of Innocence*, however, like of some of her other fiction, she avoids the problems of unsuitable mothering by having Ellen Olenska orphaned early. Like Lily Bart (*The House of Mirth*), Mattie (*Ethan Frome*), Sophie Viner (*The Reef*), and Charity Royall (*Summer*), Ellen has no one to rely on for the kind of full acceptance a mother might provide. In some of Wharton's works, the loss of the mother creates independence; more often it leads to lonely confusion. The narratives of many of Wharton's motherless women are searches for the comfort and confidence a parent's love could supply.

When Wharton does portray a close mother-daughter bond, she often uses the relationship either to mock or to warn. In the case of Janey and Mrs. Archer, "Mrs. and Miss Archer" (33), Wharton satirizes their close dependence. She shows Janey's warped sense of society, and she suggests that both women's adoration of Newland has given him the superiority complex that keeps him from being as acute an observer as he needs to be. In their West 28th Street home, the "upper floor was dedicated to Newland, and the two women squeezed themselves into narrower quarters below. In an unclouded harmony of tastes and interests they cultivated ferns in Wardian cases, made macramé lace and wool embroidery on linen, collected American revolutionary glazed ware, subscribed to 'Good Words,' and read Ouida's novels for the sake of the Italian atmosphere" (33).

What is most chilling about the two women is their likeness: "The long habit of living together in mutually dependent intimacy had given them the same vocabulary, and the same habit of beginning their phrases 'Mother thinks' or 'Janey thinks,' according as one or the other wished to advance an opinion of her own" (34). Even as Newland tries to resist becoming part of this stultifying life, it is from his mother that he has learned the rules of intimate communication. For the upper-class society Wharton draws is one that avoids anything unsightly by silencing it out of existence. To admit in language was to acknowledge: as Wharton notes, "it was against all the rules of their code that mother and son should ever allude to what was uppermost in their thoughts" (37).

As the author defines mothering, this imparting of information, of good advice, seems to be central to the parental role. Mothers are to be sources of valid information. In this respect, Ellen Olenska is doubly handicapped: not only has she lost her mother, but Medora Manson, a mother substitute, is so foolish that Ellen must become her mother—managing both finances and affairs of the heart for the older woman.

May Welland, then, has the advantage of a mother who certainly is a veritable fountain of good advice. Wharton shows the reader the depth of the bond between Augusta Welland and her daughter in scenes that describe both their physical closeness and their unity of ambition. For example, in the betrothal scene, Newland enters the Beauforts' drawing room to find

> Mrs. Welland and her daughter standing near the ball-room door. Couples were already gliding over the floor beyond. . . . Miss Welland, evidently about to join the dancers, hung on the threshold, her lilies-of-the-valley in her hand (she carried no other bouquet), her face a little pale, her eyes burning with a candid excitement. A group of young men and girls were gathered about her, and there was much hand-clasping, laughing and pleasantry on which Mrs. Welland, standing slightly apart, shed the beam of a qualified approval. It was evident that Miss Welland was in the act of announcing her engagement, while her mother affected the air of parental reluctance considered suitable to the occasion. (22)

Making clear that Newland feels himself to be an outsider, some extra appendage to the announcement ritual, Wharton continues to emphasize the mother-daughter collusion. Both have their roles in this drama, and both play them well. May's is to announce blushingly, Augusta's is to be reluctant, to move aside. But Wharton makes it obvious that the scene belongs to the two women: Newland is not in the picture at all.

She also emphasizes the patronymic names ("Mrs. Welland" is rarely referred to as "Augusta," just as Mrs. Archer rarely appears as "Adeline"), further underscoring the position of the women as members of a family, a tribe. The juxtaposing of the two opening sentences of the quotation above suggests that May and her mother are joined as if they were a couple. Newland, feeling left out, claims May for a dance as if he were only a suitor. Wharton's description suggests more than a little that the engagement triumph belongs, perhaps rightly, to the Welland women.

Wharton's choice of the name Welland (with its slant rhyme to Newland) also suggests that the stereotypical notions which govern New York society are healthful. What could be more sanguine than to live in a land where all is "well"? That the Welland clan can easily absorb the spirit suggested by the author's choice of Newland as her protagonist's Christian name (which is also his mother's family name) is borne out in the course of the narrative. Whatever was avant-garde about Archer is quickly muted by his marriage, despite May's condescension during their courtship: "'Newland! You're so original!'" (82). The sonority of this group of names (Welland, Archer, van der Luyden) sits strangely with that of the Countess Olenska. "Foreign" to the staid New Yorkers in every way, Ellen Mingott is even criticized from an unlikely quarter as Janey Archer querulously suggests she might have called herself "Elaine" rather than keeping her "ugly" American name, Ellen. Her mother's rejoinder is swift: "'It sounds more conspicuous; and that can hardly be what she wishes,' said Mrs. Archer distantly" (40). Newland tries to defend the countess, asking "'Why shouldn't she be conspicuous if she chooses? Why should she slink about as if it were she who had disgraced herself? She's "poor Ellen" certainly, because she had the bad luck to make a wretched marriage; but I don't see that that's a reason for hiding her head as if she were the culprit'" (40). The silence and changes of subject that greet his impassioned reply reinforce once again the power of the delineation of the unspeakable. Ellen Olenska, in many ways, is not to be countenanced.

Nor is her story. With her polished artistry, Wharton makes good use of Ellen's exotic name in the early scene when Newland attempts to comfort her as she sobs over her supposedly supportive family's unwillingness to deal with her tragic history—or even to listen to it.

> "Madame Olenska!—Oh, don't, Ellen," he cried, starting up and bending over her. He drew down one of her hands, clasping and chafing it like a child's while he murmured reassuring words; but in a moment she freed herself, and looked up at him with her wet lashes. "Does no one cry here, either? I suppose there's no need to, in heaven," she said, straightening her loosened braids with a laugh. . . . It was burnt into his consciousness that he had called her "Ellen"—called her so twice. . . . (77)

While the scene furthers the romance plot, as the reader sees how emotionally involved Newland already is, it also encapsulates the real vacuity of the society Ellen is trying to enter.

When Newland tells her, for instance, that "the older women, your Granny Mingott, Mrs. Welland, Mrs. van der Luyden. They like and admire you—they want to help you" (77), she corrects him:

> "Oh, I know—I know! But on condition that they don't hear any-
> thing unpleasant. Aunt Welland put it in those very words when I
> tried. . . . Does no one want to know the truth here, Mr. Archer?
> The real loneliness is living among all these kind people who only
> ask one to pretend!" (77)

If her women relatives—the people closest to her and seemingly most interested in her well-being—cannot bear to hear anything about her sad past, then Ellen loses those years of her existence. To silence Ellen, to erase the experiences that have made her the woman she is, is to change her into someone other. The cruelest kind of "help" is that which defines reality out of existence.

That Wharton chooses to emphasize this quality of the culture reflects her own experience, her bewilderment at her mother's ten-dency to silence her during important conversations. From early childhood, when she was told "'You're too little to understand,' or else 'It's not nice to ask about such things,'" Wharton felt that noth-ing she wanted to know was proper. She recalls in her memoir, she had "a penetrating sense of 'not-niceness'" that left her so ignorant about sex she knew nothing about it "till I had been married for sev-eral weeks." The often-recounted narrative of Edith Jones's asking her mother for information about the sex act a few days before her wedding bears repeating:

> I summoned up courage to appeal to my mother, & begged her,
> with a heart beating to suffocation, to tell me "what being mar-
> ried was like." Her handsome face at once took on the look of
> icy disapproval which I most dreaded. "I never heard such a
> ridiculous question!" she said impatiently; & I felt at once how
> vulgar she thought me. But in the extremity of my need I per-
> sisted. "I'm afraid, Mamma—I want to know what will happen
> to me!" The coldness of her expression deepened to disgust. She
> was silent for a dreadful moment; then she said with an effort:

"You've seen enough pictures & statues in your life. Haven't you noticed that men are—made differently from women?"

"Yes," I faltered blankly.

"Well, then—?"

I was silent, from sheer inability to follow, & she brought out sharply: "Then for heaven's sake don't ask me any more silly questions. You can't be as stupid as you pretend!" (*LI*, 1087–88)

From the retrospective view of her memoir, Wharton glosses the poignant conversation. Being thought "vulgar" and "stupid" were the crosses of Edith Jones' life (notice how acerbic May is when she reminds Newland that his behavior is "vulgar"). Wharton concludes her narrative about her mother's failure to give her anything other than insults: "I record this brief conversation, because the training of which it was the beautiful & logical conclusion did more than anything else to falsify & misdirect my whole life."

"The age of innocence" might have been better named "the age of misinformation." With this indictment, Wharton connects some of the elliptical scenes having to do with language and its power into an even more critical narrative than the reader might expect. Whenever Ellen tries to say anything, she is faced with the stolid, closed faces of the society that denies her expression. Perhaps Newland's charm for her is that he does appear to listen—to a point. But Wharton's emphasis is on the failure of the women characters, rather than on Ellen's finding possible solace; and in her depiction of failure, even Catherine Mingott comes in for criticism.

The reader becomes suspicious of Catherine's vaunted independence and wisdom early on, when she jokingly asks Newland why he didn't marry Ellen instead of May. For whatever reason, this inquiry makes little sense. It might be a means of praising her black-sheep granddaughter, Ellen, but for Newland to change his life partner means irretrievably harming May, who is Catherine's other granddaughter. Skeptical of Catherine's real intentions, the reader is not surprised when she, like the rest of the family, turns against Ellen. Catherine's disapproval is even more visible because she withholds crucial monetary support.

Catherine also disappoints the reader when she rejects Regina Beaufort's plea for her financial help—and is so horrified by that woman's "vulgar" behavior that she suffers a stroke in reaction. Wharton is clearly showing that even the most powerful and idiosyncratic women characters are part and parcel of the society they supposedly disdain. It matters little that Catherine, late in the book, admits her stupidity and tells Newland that she has been wrong about Ellen.

> "Well, it's settled, anyhow: she's going to stay with me, whatever the rest of the family say! She hadn't been here five minutes before I'd have gone down on my knees to keep her. . . . "They'd talked me over, as no doubt you know: persuaded me, Lovell, and Letterblair, and Augusta Welland, and all the rest of them, that I must hold out and cut off her allowance, till she was made to see that it was her duty to go back to Olenski. They thought they'd convinced me when the secretary, or whatever he was, came out with the last proposals: handsome proposals I confess they were. After all, marriage is marriage, and money's money—both useful things in their way . . . and I didn't know what to answer. . . . But the minute I laid eyes on her, I said: 'You sweet bird, you! Shut you up in that cage again? Never!'" (299–300)

Her admission comes too late and is made to the wrong person. It also is made to enlist Newland's help: "we shall have a fight yet. The family don't want her here" (301).

As the most likely mother substitute for Ellen, Catherine Spicer Mingott too is a failure. This is a more severe blow to Ellen's expectations of what being part of a family means than the defections of her other relatives. After all, Ellen says early on that she has returned to her family because "I want to feel cared for and safe" (73). But her life as a New Yorker is effectively ended by the unified defection of the Family (spelled with a capital letter, as it is by Newland near the end of the novel), which is evident in the farewell dinner given for Ellen by her loving cousin May.

As she approaches the final scene of Ellen's attempting to interact with the family tribunal, to no avail, Wharton becomes more explicit about the power of that family. "There were certain things that had to be done, and if done at all, done handsomely and thoroughly; and one of these, in the old New York code, was the tribal rally around a kinswoman about to be eliminated from the tribe" (334). Placed at the center of them all, an obvious part of "the conspiracy," Newland finally sees that "the whole tribe had rallied about his wife on the tacit assumption that nobody knew anything, or had ever imagined anything, and that the occasion of the entertainment was simply May Archer's natural desire to take an affectionate leave of her friend and cousin" (335).

For the first time in the book, Wharton uses May's married name, her position as legal wife giving her the wherewithal to banish her rival. Earlier, the author makes clear that May and her mother had planned the dinner, had in fact addressed the invitations, long before Newland had been apprised of the existence of either plans or dinner. Once again this timing, which parallels that of both the announcement of his and May's engagement and May's pregnancy, leaves Newland outside the intimate circle of those who know.

Wharton's most didactic statement of what was occurring at the dinner comes later: "It was the old New York way of taking life 'without effusion of blood': the way of people who dreaded scandal more than disease, who placed decency above courage, and who considered that nothing was more ill-bred than 'scenes,' except the behaviour of those who gave rise to them" (335).

But her most subtle finale comes at the close of the dinner, when the reader's attention is riveted on Newland, expecting that he will make some gesture, some response, to the calm pain with which Ellen has survived the ordeal. Then, almost beyond Newland's vision, May continues to play the role of admiring young cousin to the older Ellen as she and Ellen enact what is surely intended to suggest a primitive ritual:

> She [Ellen] went up to May, the rest of the company making a circle about her as she advanced. The two young women clasped hands; then May bent forward and kissed her cousin. (340)

Newland's stunned recognition of his wife's Judas-like kiss echoes that of the reader. Wharton moves abruptly into a sequence of Larry Lefferts' implicating Archer in his own adulteries, as if to diminish the importance of what has just happened to Ellen at the hands of her family. But she might have juxtaposed two scenes from earlier in the novel: one, as Newland asks himself "if May's face was doomed to thicken into the same middle-aged image of invincible innocence" as her mother's (145); the other, as he recognizes the vestiges of pain in Ellen Olenska: "It frightened him to think what must have gone to the making of her eyes" (62).

Given Newland's sometimes superior ability to see through the social facades that the rest of his community accepts, Wharton never lets him gain the status of hero. The reader is reminded of his cutting criticism of the very family that eventually will best him, in a scene in which he takes on his mother and sister. His position is that Ellen Olenska has the right to do whatever she wants, but Janey warns him,

> "You're marrying into her family."
> "Oh, family—family!" he jeered.
> "Newland—don't you care about Family?"
> "Not a brass farthing."
> "Nor about what cousin Louisa van der Luyden will think?"
> "Not the half of one—if she thinks such old maid's rubbish."
> "Mother is not an old maid," said his virgin sister with pinched lips. He felt like shouting back: "Yes, she is, and so are the van der Luydens, and so we all are, when it comes to being so much as brushed by the wing-tip of Reality." But he saw her long gentle face puckering into tears, and felt ashamed of the useless pain he was inflicting.
> "Hang Countess Olenska! Don't be a goose, Janey—I'm not her keeper." (85)

It would be too glib to suggest, of course, that it (Family) actually hangs Ellen, because Wharton's movement between what Newland wants to say and what he does say, salving his old maid sister's feelings rather than affronting them further, parallels other scenes in which Wharton repeats this technique. For all his sometimes imperious independence, Newland finally cannot say what is in his heart. He is as much a part of this society and of all the families included in "their" community as the rest of his family, and the poignance of his having to renounce his love for Ellen is that his ties to community are the strongest part of his nature.

Or, as his maligned but powerful mother says early in the novel, "we belong here, and people should respect our ways when they come among us" (87).

12

Old New York: Wharton's Postscript to *The Age of Innocence*

Although Wharton was pleased with what she had accomplished in her 1920 novel, she had not completely written out her anger and resentment at the social code that governed women's behavior in American society. For the privilege of belonging, any woman had to accept conditions that not only circumscribed her independence, but also forced her into male-dependent roles. Good women in old New York society were either daughters or wives; and Wharton, after her divorce and her father's death, was neither.

When she uses the phrase "old New York" in her devastating comment about tribal bloodletting, Wharton reminds the reader that she had originally chosen that phrase as the title of *The Age of Innocence*. She was to use it several years later as the title for the group of four novellas she began writing as soon as she had completed the novel. In 1921, then, Wharton worked concurrently on the intentionally light novel, *The Glimpses of the Moon,* a parodic revisiting of *The House of Mirth* in its scrutiny of marriage as social rite, and "The Old Maid," her powerful work about an out-of-wedlock birth that changes the passionate Charlotte Lovell into an apparent old maid. Foreshadowing her much later story "Roman Fever," this novella works much more intricately with issues of family pride, possessorship, and women's susceptibility to both first loves and motherhood.

Set in the 1850s, "The Old Maid" draws on the same social matrix as *The Age of Innocence*; in fact, as Shari Benstock notes, it was the first of what Wharton planned to be two novellas titled "Among the Mingotts." For it Wharton borrowed from the extensive genealogy of the Mingott and Manson families, which she had drawn in her notes for *The Age of Innocence*.[1] In the narrative of the unmarried Charlotte Lovell, who gives birth to a daughter as a result of her affair with an "unsuitable" lover (a man in love with her married cousin, Delia), Wharton continues her sympathetic treatment of women of passion. Like Charity in *Summer,* Charlotte is willing to take on the shame of Clementina's birth, and the care of the child, so long as the memory of her love with Clement Spencer endures.

Unfortunately, when Charlotte succumbs to her other desire—to be married and a part of the New York society her friends inhabit—she confesses her past to her cousin Delia. In what seems to be a much more kindly depiction of cousins' friendship, Wharton actually re-inscribes May's betrayal of Ellen Olenska: Delia convinces her husband to allow her to take the young child, but as a penalty for Charlotte, Delia tells her cousin's fiancé that Charlotte is breaking the engagement. Rather than having it all—security for her child, marriage, and secrecy about her past—Charlotte must give up marriage. She then becomes "the old maid."

As Wharton works through the next 20 years of the women's forming a household and struggling over which one is to play the role of mother to Tina, the reader is struck by the similarities between the novella and *The Age of Innocence*. Intent on observing social forms, the society Delia represents cares little for truth. When she goes to the wise doctor to ask him whether or not she should legally adopt Tina (because without family income, the young woman will never find a respectable husband), she learns that her seemingly trusting husband had visited the doctor years before, needing to know whose child the foundling was before he acquiesced to Delia's taking it. Delia learns what Wharton had long suspected, that no woman ever has the power she thinks is hers.

At the end of the novella, on the evening before Tina's marriage to the man she loves (able now to marry her because of her adoption/fortune), both Delia and Charlotte prove themselves to be better people than they had seemed. Charlotte gives up her right as the real mother to have the last moments alone with her child, and Delia in turn asks Tina to save her last kiss for her Aunt Charlotte. The reader is reminded of Wharton's comment in *The Writing of Fiction* as she discusses the importance of the selection of "crucial moments," those that "need not involve action in the sense of external events. . . . But there must be something that makes them crucial" (*Writing*, 13).

Wharton's second novella, "New Year's Day," not only includes these crucial moments, it consists largely of them. A fire at the Fifth Avenue Hotel exposes a tryst between the beautiful Mrs. Hazeldean and the wealthy Henry Prest. "'She was bad . . . always. They used to meet at the Fifth Avenue Hotel,' said my mother . . . how the precision of the phrase characterized my old New York!" Although the actions of a seemingly unfaithful wife form the plot of this work, Wharton creates more reader interest by having it narrated by an adolescent boy. His attitudes are set against those of his judgmental mother (i.e., he notes that "it was typical of my mother to be always employed in benevolent actions while she uttered uncharitable words").[2]

Beyond using the boy's innocence as a vehicle to puncture the self-righteousness of New York culture, Wharton devotes most of her attention to re-creating Lizzie Hazeldean's guilt as she hastens home from the hotel. What Wharton does here so well is undercut the character of Mrs. Hazeldean as promiscuous. Though she describes her watchful behavior as practiced, second nature to "a woman in her situation" (499), Wharton leaves no doubt that her protagonist deeply loves her husband, ailing and impoverished though he is.

Lizzie Hazeldean, too, wears a diamond-tipped golden arrow in her hair. With this signal, Wharton ironically foreshadows the unexpected denouement—that her protagonist has the affair with Prest precisely to keep her marriage intact. For her love of her husband, she becomes Prest's mistress. Although society would judge her and May

Welland to be opposites, Wharton compares them as strong women, intent on preserving their marriages.

For her infidelity—no matter what its rationale—Lizzie spends the rest of her life, after Charlie's death, in the isolation of the fallen woman. Refusing Prest's subsequent proposal, she chooses the state of being thought promiscuous over becoming a legitimate, and therefore powerful, wife. In "New Year's Day," then, Wharton gives Ellen Olenska's probable tryst with Newland (had that meeting ever occurred) the outcome that New York society would have expected.

Unexpectedly profitable, both novellas were sold to *Redbook* ("The Old Maid" was initially refused by *Ladies' Home Journal* on the grounds that its subject matter was objectionable). The first brought in over $2,000, and "New Year's Day," $6,000. Neither of the remaining novellas was as successful; "False Dawn" and "Sparks" lack the sense of the genuine that Wharton captures in both "The Old Maid" and "New Year's Day."

Both novellas deal more generally with male characters, and more predictably with the conflicts between an artistic sensibility and one given to making money. An old theme in American letters, it was treated thoroughly by both Hawthorne and Melville; Wharton's attempts to characterize old New York by focusing on the pursuits of male characters who are simplified to be either "materialist" or "aesthetic" are less successful than the first two novellas in the collection.

In "False Dawn," Wharton writes about artistic taste in conflict with family/patriarchal coercion. A son, sent abroad for his Grand Tour, is asked to purchase oils for a gallery that will carry the family name. Disappointed in the modernity of the paintings (which have been selected with the advice of John Ruskin, Dante Rosetti, and others of their circle), the father disowns his heir. Generations later the collection is discovered in the attic of a distant relative, and given its proper value. "The Spark" is also a more literary tale, focusing on the influence the poet Walt Whitman has had on an unlearned, and somewhat materialistic, New Yorker. Though Wharton explains that the latter is not really a story, attempting some postmodernist innovation in the telling of the tale, the narrative seems to have little relevance to most of the themes she had been working through.

As narratives that filled in the spaces in her *Old New York* collection, published in 1924 to large sales, the tales are adequate and satisfying. Neither of them has the comparatively impassioned energy of "The Old Maid" and "New Year's Day," novellas that complete, or at least complement, Wharton's themes from *The Age of Innocence*. The difference in the two sets of stories seems to illustrate her wisdom when she writes in *The Writing of Fiction* that the chief quality the writer must cultivate is the "creative imagination." Sympathy alone is not enough. Neither is any mechanical "understanding" of situations. For Wharton, the creative imagination "combines with the power of penetrating into other minds that of standing far enough aloof for them to see beyond" (*Writing*, 15).

Such imagining is not based only on autobiographical knowledge, although the author does admit that "As to experience, intellectual and moral, the creative imagination can make a little go a long way, provided it remains long enough in the mind and is sufficiently brooded upon. One good heart-break will furnish the poet with many songs, and the novelist with a considerable number of novels. But they must have hearts that can break" (*Writing*, 21). To oversimplify, Wharton cared about the women characters who populate "The Old Maid" and "New Year's Day"; she had known the kind of tension, shame, and love that their respective stories told. Although she might have had excellent taste in art, and we know she cared about Whitman's writing, these intellectual absorptions do not demand the same level of emotional involvement.

13

The Oasis of Nostalgia

There is little question that Edith Wharton mellowed with age. As many of her closest friends and household companions died, as she achieved the kind of fame she had long dreamed of having, she grew in some ways more outspoken (witness the truly sensational topics of *The Mother's Recompense, Twilight Sleep* and *The Children*) but in others, kinder.

If Wharton were to return to the period of time when she was composing *The Age of Innocence,* and approach its themes once more with the wisdom and gentleness she exhibits at the close of her career, she might structure the novel differently. Her animosity toward Newland Archer's lack of energy might be softened with a section of exposition in which she presents his boyhood, his growing up without a father in the stultifying culture of the brownstone, which is so dominated by his mother and sister that he can barely escape to his second floor without some interference by them. Just as Janey sits up to see what May's telegram says, so every letter that arrives, every visitor to their home, is the province of Mrs. and Miss Archer. They in effect screen everything before Newland sees it. As Wharton makes clear, a good bit of his seemingly modern behavior (making statements he knows will shock his family, having the affair with Mrs. Rushworth) stems from his delight in upsetting the good women who in reality rule the household.

Perhaps Newland's tendency to respect the aging Sillerton Jackson, like his need to be accepted by his male peer group—even to the extent of being complicit in its adulteries—also relates to his isolation in what appears to be a female world. With such contextualization, Wharton might easily have evoked more sympathy for Newland.

As it was, according to her notes for the novel, she was intent from the start on making him a weak protagonist. Named first "Langdon" and then "Lawrence," Archer was clearly to be another man like Lawrence Selden, who arrived with too little, too late. Although Wharton knew Ellen was not going to die as Lily Bart does, the image of the man who loves the woman in question—soothing his conscience with the thought that he had been planning to do the right thing, a thought more vapid than comforting in the presence of her dead body—transfers easily to Archer. His confusion at the time of May's farewell dinner for Ellen, his inability to say anything meaningful to her, and his equally resonant inability to say anything at all to May in the episode that follows the dinner scene marks him as the same kind of ineffectual male. When Wharton transfers powerful speech from Archer to his previously inarticulate wife, she shows clearly that the balance of power within the marriage has shifted irretrievably. Good intentions, arrived at late and inappropriately, do not constitute the behavior of a hero.

Had Wharton followed her notes for the novel, however, Newland would have been even less powerful. One of the most chilling moments occurs in Wharton's outline for the second version of the plot, when Newland is so shocked by Ellen's sexual prowess that he withdraws. When he and Ellen run away to "some little place in Florida," evidently an exotic location for trysts during the late 19th century, Wharton notes "(contrast between bridal night with May & this one). Archer is fascinated & yet terrified."[1] Chagrined by his own lack of passion, and realizing "He cannot live without New York and respectability" (26), the two return to New York separately. The affair is finished.

In her notes for the first plan of the novel, Wharton makes Newland even more of a passive lover. In this version, he breaks his engagement to May and marries Ellen. But when they return from their European honeymoon, she cannot face the rest of her life lived as his wife, within that New York culture: "her whole soul recoils" (24). Ellen, then, goes to live in Europe. They remain married, although "Archer consents to a separation. He realizes dimly that there is no use struggling with her. He arranges his own life as best he can, & occasionally goes to Europe, & usually calls on his wife, & is asked to dine with her. She is very poor, & very lonely, but she has a real life." Wharton's conclusion to this plan is often quoted: she says of Newland, living again with his mother and sister, that "nothing ever happens to him again" (24).

In the author's notes for all three versions of the novel, emphasis falls repeatedly on the passion Ellen feels about living in Europe. Ellen, here named Clementina or Clementine (as was the illegitimate daughter in "The Old Maid"), decides she cannot live "without Europe and emotion" (26). Similarly, in Wharton's third plan, after their liaison in Florida (which follows what Wharton calls Newland's "tame colourless and eminently respectable wedding trip" with May), "Archer realizes that he cannot break with society & live as an outcast with [cancelled: an 'immor[al]'] another man's wife. Mme. Olenska, on her side, is weary of their sentimental tête à tête & his scruples" (27). As Wharton writes this description, there is nothing remotely positive about Ellen's feeling for Newland. Even in her infatuated eyes, he becomes the stolid bore his culture has created—and a sentimental one at that.

Wharton's recasting of the protagonists in what becomes the actual novel, then, goes a long way to soften the negative effects of Newland's self-satisfied yet always weak ardor. Just as Ellen becomes much more innocent, so Newland becomes much more capable of love—and of being loved. The narrative charts a romance that the reader believes, most of the time, is real, possible, impassioned—and it does so chiefly through Wharton's use of apt ellipses that leave much to the reader's imagination.

In the context of Wharton's early notes for the novel, then, the troublesome ending portrays Ellen Olenska as much less pathetic than some readers have characterized her as being. Rather than a woman who has relinquished her only love and lived most of her adult life alone, Ellen might well be the person who has had "a real life," the person Newland imagines as inseparable from the exotic Parisian setting: "For nearly thirty years, her life—of which he knew so strangely little—had been spent in this rich atmosphere that he already felt to be too dense and yet too stimulating for his lungs" (359). As he envisions this rich atmosphere, Wharton writes in loving cadences of "the radiant outbreak of spring down the avenues of horse-chestnuts, the flowers and statues in the public gardens, the whiff of lilacs from the flower-carts, the majestic roll of the river under the great bridges, and the life of art and study and pleasure that filled each mighty artery to bursting" (354).

A few recent readings of *The Age of Innocence* see Newland's imaging of Ellen's later life as only rhetoric. That imaging lets him off the hook, and dodges the question of what Ellen's life in Paris (for nearly 30 years) had really been. Structurally, there is no way for the reader to know about Ellen's life. Wharton purposely avoids having to tell that story—perhaps the account of her own sometimes lonely years after her divorce and self-expatriation, watching good friends return to the United States or die, lingering too often at the edge of a younger crowd.

The role of the reader, however, is to fill gaps; and Wharton leaves the reader that obvious silence about Ellen's years in Paris. Given the direction of the author's notes for the novel, supplemented with her explicit descriptions of the country she chose as home once she was free of her marriage, the reader might be convinced that Ellen Olenska has been happy, has been satisfied with what was, truly, an interesting life. In this context, Newland's description of himself becomes more poignant: "he felt shy, old-fashioned, inadequate: a mere grey speck of a man compared with the ruthless magnificent fellow he had dreamed of being" (354).

Shari Benstock says it best: "Edith Wharton wanted a *French* life." As Benstock explains all the excuses the author used even while she was still providing for Teddy's happiness and support, she had "found there [in Paris] an intellectual, artistic, and cultural milieu in which she moved with ease. She was to spend the next thirteen years of her life in this city, later moving to the French countryside; her expatriation in France continued until her death in 1937. Before taking up official residence in France, however, she studied carefully the society she was later to conquer, she learned its history and literature, she made extensive journeys between its borders, she shed those vestiges of Americanism that her future compatriots might find *impétueux*, she practiced her new role as salon hostess, all the while summoning the courage to make an important break with her past. Aware that her success or failure would turn on the nuances of social form, Edith Wharton turned her energies in the early years of this century to mastering the idiosyncrasies of French protocol in the Faubourg St. Germain."[2] Like Ellen, who makes choices that reflect her truly individual, independent preferences, Wharton wove her single choices into the fabric of life she desired. She was comfortable with those choices. She writes later in *A Backward Glance,* "I was old, I was alone, and I had learned the necessity of living within one's means. . . . But I am born happy every morning . . . the days have a way of being jubilant" (*ABG,* 1058–59).

Wharton wanted the French, cosmopolitan life, but she also, in her proud way, wanted to re-create what might have been her existence had she made other choices. In her figuration of Ellen Olenska, she not only inscribes her own choices and tastes—always played off against the traditional New York choices and tastes exemplified by Newland Archer—but she also links the character of Ellen to the matriarchy of strong and independent women who populate other of her fictions. It is difficult for the reader to understand Ellen at all without first having learned the strength of Catherine Mingott. Just as she continued writing the narrative of "Mrs. Manson Mingott" in "The Old Maid," by frequent comparisons between that powerful woman and her granddaughter Delia Ralston, so Wharton found herself intrigued by women who had lived, and made their reputations, through their own often unconventional choices.

Wharton was in her late 50s when she wrote *The Age of Innocence.* The history of her writing career shows that she was already planning to write memoirs of her childhood and adolescence, and her experiences with Fullerton; it seems likely that she had recently written the lushly detailed "Beatrice Palmato" father-daughter incest fragment. Although her friends may not have known that her health was failing, Wharton knew; and she was realistic enough to see that she would eventually have to at least curtail her work. It therefore seems reasonable that she would have considered the writing of *The Age of Innocence* a way back to the sources, the life, that held much more than nostalgic interest for her because she was so happy with the woman she had become—especially when she considered what a fragile, susceptible, and easily influenced child she had been. Writing this novel was, for her, a way back into what she was to call "the secret story-world in which I lived" (*LI*, 1077).

Instead of "nostalgia," then, perhaps a better way of describing why Wharton wrote about New York during the 1870s was "self-exploration." Rushed as she had been throughout the years of The Great War, recently honored for both her war efforts and her lifetime career as a writer, Wharton was poised for both rest and a true kind of recuperation, the recuperation of those life experiences that had made her into the woman she was, the woman so capable and feisty that the men she thought her intellectual equals were often daunted by her physical and mental achievements.

Ellen Olenska, the outsider, the woman who remains inexplicable (intentionally and purposefully, carefully drawn to be so by Wharton the consummate writer), is in some ways a self-portrait. Through the layers of self-fashioning that every person builds in shaping autobiography, Wharton tried to dissect character, tried to show traits that would ultimately lead Ellen to the outcome the novel presents. Such an exercise was satisfying on a personal level, surely; but it also gave rise to a figure that remains enigmatic. No reader is sure what Ellen feels at the end of *The Age of Innocence*; no reader wants to explain why Ellen is able to leave the dinner, and to accept May's kiss, without rancor or even visible distress. Instead, readers turn (for a kind of relief) to assessing what Newland feels, and wants, and does. The existence of what is, finally, a self-protective narrative strategy suggests in itself that Wharton was deeply involved in the creation of Ellen Olenska.

She would have enjoyed Grace Kellogg's evaluation of the mysterious Ellen, then, as a woman "lovely not only in the flesh, but in her quick spirit, in the generous impulses of her heart."[3] And she would have understood Mary Ellis Gibson's somewhat tentative judgment about *The Age of Innocence* entire. Gibson points out that the book shows "that restrictive conventions may be the price of traditional stabilty. No one would wish to become Newland Archer, with his ineffectual dreams of passion. . . . The novel itself is an act of ironic poise, the poise of a longing . . . for what one would not wholly have wished to have."[4]

Wharton's signal to the reader that relinquishment of even a great love may be less than the grandest of narrative plots comes through her sly title. It might seem as if *The Age of Innocence* is a positive marking, but who among her readers in 1920 was set to value innocence? What is innocence but a vacuum in experience? How can one remain innocent of anything, if one observes, moves out into life, experiences? Not for nothing had Wharton met Bronislaw Malinowski—she understood the concept of anthropological study, and she was willing to use this concept, up to a point. But what she really understood was the age-old appeal of a good, heavily emotional, romantic story. As she states in *The Writing of Fiction*, "Modern fiction really began when the 'action' of the novel was transferred from the street to the soul." She uses Madame de La Fayette's *La Princesse de Cléves* as the example of modern fiction, describing the work as "a story of hopeless love and mute renunciation in which the stately tenor of the lives depicted is hardly ruffled by the exultations and agonies succeeding each other below the surface" (*Writing*, 3). Wryly, with the same kind of tongue-in-cheek wit for which she was known among her friends, Wharton here describes her own *The Age of Innocence*.

As we have seen, even while she seems to valorize innocence, she attacks the premise that such a quality is in any way admirable, healthful, or wise. She gives the reader Janey Archer, stifled, separated from any kind of natural growth. She gives us May Welland, so controlled by the social forms that govern her life that she gives up both genuine feeling and honesty—the hallmark for Wharton of a truly noble character. She gives us a society built only on facades, while essential human values go unrecognized and unrewarded.

Wharton wrote *The Age of Innocence,* in part, to take her mind off the ravages and waste of World War I. She wrote it also as a means of establishing, for her own satisfaction, how she had become the woman she was. And she probably wrote it, again with some mixture of irony and wit, to pay tribute to the writer she claimed was never a primary influence (but who, of course, was): Henry James.

As Cynthia Griffin Wolff has explained, throughout this novel Wharton plays a set of intertextual games with James and his work. The tellingly innocent Newland Archer has a number of similarities with both such Jamesian heroes as Christopher Newman (*The American*) and such heroines as Isabel Archer (*The Portrait of a Lady*), with both of whom Newland obviously shares a name. Wolff notes that a friend's remark to him ("'You're like the pictures on the walls of a deserted house: "The Portrait of a Gentleman"'") makes clear that "Newland Archer is intended as a parallel to Isabel Archer."[5] Furthermore, *The Age of Innocence* is the title of not only Wharton's novel, but of a well-known portrait by Reynolds hung in the National Gallery. The Reynolds painting is, literally, the portrait of a lady, a very young girl.

The most personal touch of all, according to Wolff, is the ending scene of the book, when Newland looks up at the balcony as light fails, seeing not the figure of the woman he once loved but the manservant with a light. As Wharton well knew, one of the most moving of James's experiences near the end of his life was the epiphanic moment when he stood alone on the pavement, watching lights being lit on a third story balcony, and straining through his unexpected tears to see the "unapproachable face" that he knew was there. He never saw the face, although he stood in the spot for hours.[6]

There is little reason to think that Wharton drew Newland Archer specifically to link that character with Henry James, but both are also fastidious men in search of elusive physical comfort. As Wendy Gimbel points out, Newland is a person never satisfied with another's living space. He is uncomfortable in the Wellands' house, in May's replica of their house in his own, in Ellen's strangely furnished rooms, and even in his own second-floor study.[7] Perhaps what would have made Newland happiest in life was not Ellen Olenska at all, but his own carefully chosen and tastefully furnished space. Considering the struggle Henry James had with his family over his purchase of Lamb House,[8] Wharton may have created another correspondence for readers who had known James. And her own recognition that personal space is a more enduring solace than the romance of even a great love may have been one of the determining beliefs of Wharton's late life and writing.

It goes a long way in explaining Kate Clephane's choices in *The Mother's Recompense*. It goes at least part way in explaining Lizzie Hazeldean's choices in "New Year's Day" and, for that matter, those of the unpolished, aging man whose life has been so influenced by Whitman in "The Spark." Although more difficult to name, it might also explain the generosity of both Delia and Charlotte in "The Old Maid."

For it is in this novella, written shortly after Wharton had finished *The Age of Innocence,* that she makes her sharpest comments about the supposedly blissful state of "marriage" as young women of her culture were supposed to experience it. The sexual text nearly absent from Wharton's published fiction makes its appearance here, as Delia Ralston relives the intimacy of her wedded state:

> There was the startled puzzled surrender to the incomprehensible exigencies of the young man to whom one had at most yielded a rosy cheek in return for an engagement ring; there was the large double-bed; the terror of seeing him shaving calmly the next morning, in his shirtsleeves, through the dressing-room door; . . . a week or a month of flushed distress, confusion, embarrassed pleasure; then the growth of habit, the insidious lulling of the matter-of-course, the dreamless double slumbers in the big white bed, the early morning discussions and consultations through that dressing-room door which had once seemed to open into a fiery pit scorching the brow of innocence.[9]

Wharton's choice of the word *terror* speaks volumes. She hardly needs to return at the end of the passage to the image of sexual knowledge, the sight of the male body, scorching the innocence of exactly the kind of sheltered girl Victorian society cherished. But she goes an important step further. Once she has stepped beyond the woman's shock at the whole ritual of sexual intercourse, and its resulting intimacies, she punctures the social code again by saying bluntly, "And then, the babies; the babies who were supposed to 'make up for everything,' and didn't" (377). To clarify her intention further, she continues, "one had no definite notion as to what it was that one had missed, and that they were to make up for" (377).

Characteristic of the way Wharton's fiction often worked, as an oeuvre of separate texts, one informed by another in ways that might well remain known only to the author herself, here in "The Old Maid" she delivers her most negative and direct analysis of a woman's role in marriage. Drawing from scenes and incidents in *The Age of Innocence,* and using the word *innocence* once more, she describes a woman's terror of sex, her dislike of babies, and her angry questioning of the whole social fabric that excuses any but male rights.

What saves Delia's tranquillity, and reinforces her conformity with the very social conventions she knows she has the right to question, is her beautiful room. Within the "tall brownstone house in Gramercy Park," Delia's bedroom is her sanctuary: "the French wallpaper that reproduced a watered silk, with a 'valanced' border, and tassels between the loops. The mahogany bedstead, covered with a white embroidered counterpane, was symmetrically reflected in the mirror of a wardrobe which matched it. Coloured lithographs of the 'Four Seasons' by Léopold Robert surmounted groups of family daguerreotypes in deeply-recessed gilt frames" (377). It matters little that Wharton is satirizing Delia's taste here; what matters is that another of her strong female protagonists has found her route to survival by claiming, and furnishing, her personal space. Making up for the personal violation the rite of marriage makes necessary, Delia's room has given her boundaries, a territory in which her personal power balances her sexual powerlessness.

It is particularly interesting that her dependent cousin Charlotte also uses her choice of a room to show power. As she and Delia wrestle over which woman has the right to assume the role of mother to Clementina, Charlotte takes a room next to Tina's, thereby shutting off the girl's intimacy with her aunt but also allowing her to watch

Tina's developing fascination—and increasingly sexual behavior—with her suitor. Through the control of space, Charlotte asserts her force as Tina's mother and protector. The happy ending of her power struggle with Delia is that Charlotte does keep the headstrong girl from inevitable sexual violation. Instead, Tina remains a virgin, marries her suitor, and emerges, like May Welland, the victorious bride.

In her recasting of the classic romance, with her sometimes ironic emphasis on the (literally) thin line between virginity and promiscuity, Wharton rewrites a kind of marriage narrative that puts women characters in positions of power, and gives many of her fictions an appeal (both outright and subversive) for all generations of women readers.

For her readers in the 1920s, trained to find a male protagonist who could bear the weight of a major narrative, it was easier to read *The Age of Innocence* as a novel of manners, a story of a culture that maimed and destroyed rather than an exposé of a man who could have rediscovered the great love of his life. And so, on the one hand, Wharton wrote a marvelously evocative novel that recalls the 1870s and 1880s in "old New York." But perhaps for readers in the 1990s, *The Age of Innocence* is more likely the story of people who don't want to give up the promise of a great love, who insist on looking for passion, who model their life searches after that character Wharton herself loved, Anna Karenina. Or perhaps it stands, in an equally modern pose, as a novel about people who make hard choices, for reasons they best understand, and are willing to live with the consequences of their decisions.

Notes and References

Chapter 1

1. Cynthia Griffin Wolff, "Chronology," in *Edith Wharton, Novellas and Other Writings* (New York: Library of America, 1990), 1109–10. The fullest account of Wharton's wartime activity is found in Shari Benstock's *No Gifts From Chance: A Biography of Edith Wharton* (New York: Scribner's, 1994).

2. Quoted in Wolff, "Chronology," in *Edith Wharton, Novellas and Other Writings*, 1108.

Chapter 2

1. Edith Wharton to Sinclair Lewis, 6 August 1921, in *The Letters of Edith Wharton*, eds. R. W. B. Lewis and Nancy Lewis (New York: Scribner's, 1988), 445.

2. Sinclair Lewis to Edith Wharton, 28 November 1921, in *Letters*, 448.

3. Edith Wharton to Sinclair Lewis, 27 August 1922, in *Letters*, 455.

4. Typical is Irving Howe's "Introduction: The Achievement of Edith Wharton" in *Edith Wharton, A Collection of Critical Essays*, ed. Irving Howe (Englewood Cliffs, N.J.: Prentice-Hall, 1962), 5. Edmund Wilson, similarly, calls *The Age of Innocence* Wharton's "valedictory," implying that her writing career was over (Edmund Wilson, "Justice to Edith Wharton," in the same collection, 26).

5. F. Scott Fitzgerald was one who did. See Robert A. Martin and Linda Wagner-Martin, "The Salons of Wharton's Fiction" in *"Wretched Exotic": Essays on Edith Wharton in Europe*, eds. Katherine Joslin and Alan Price (New York: Peter Lang, 1993), 97–110.

6. In her lifetime, five films were made of her novels, including a second "talkie" version of *The Age of Innocence* in 1934. The 1990s saw the pro-

duction of films of *The Children* and *Ethan Frome,* as well as the Martin Scorsese film of this novel, with Michelle Pfeiffer (Ellen), Winona Ryder (May), and Daniel Day-Lewis (Newland).

Chapter 3

1. Lillian Whiting, "Novels on the Season's List," *Springfield Republican* (5 December 1920), Magazine, 9-A; "Mrs. Wharton's Novel of Old New York," *Literary Digest* 68 (5 February 1921), 52.

2. See Kathy Miller Hadley's *In the Interstices of the Tale: Edith Wharton's Narrative Strategies* (New York: Peter Lang, 1993).

3. Henry Seidel Canby, "Our America," *New York Evening Post,* 6 November 1920, 3; William Lyon Phelps, "As Mrs. Wharton Sees Us," *New York Times Book Review,* 17 October 1920, 1, 11.

4. "The Age of Innocence," *Times Literary Supplement,* 25 November 1920, 775; "The Age of Innocence," *Spectator* 126 (8 January 1921), 55–56.

5. A. E. W. Mason, "The Age of Innocence," *Bookman* 52 (December 1920), 360–6l.

6. F. H., "The Age of Innocence," *New Republic* 24 (17 November 1920), 30l–2.

7. Canby, "Our America," 3; Carl Van Doren, "Contemporary American Novelists," *Nation* 112 (12 January 1921), 40–4l.

8. Phelps, "As Mrs. Wharton Sees Us," 11.

9. Carl Van Doren, "An Elder America," *Nation* 111 (3 November 1920), 510–11.

10. Katherine Mansfield, "Family Portraits," *Athenaeum* (London), no. 4728 (10 December 1920), 810–11.

11. Mason, "The Age of Innocence," 360–61; Canby, "Our America," 3; R. D. Townsend, "Novels Not for a Day," *Outlook* 126 (8 December 1920), 653; Frederick Watson, "The Assurance of Art," *Bookman* (London) 49 (19 January 1921), 170, 172.

12. Edwin Francis Edgett, "The Strange Case of Edith Wharton," *Boston Evening Transcript* (23 October 1920), part 4, p. 4; *Spectator,* 55–56.

13. "Mrs. Wharton's Novel of Old New York," *Literary Digest* 68 (5 February 1921), 52; and see "The Innocence of New York," *Saturday Review* (London) 80 (4 December 1920), 458.

14. Vernon L. Parrington, "Our Literary Aristocrat," *The Pacific Review* 2 (June 1921), 157–60; 157.

15. Arthur Hobson Quinn, "Edith Wharton" (pamphlet, n.d.), quoted in Katherine Joslin, "Edith Wharton at 125," *College Literature* 14, no. 3 (1987), 205.

Notes and References

16. Edith Wharton to Sinclair Lewis, 6 August 1921, in *Letters*, 445.

17. Edmund Wilson, "Justice to Edith Wharton," *The Wound and the Bow* (New York: Oxford University Press, 1947), 195–213; 208.

18. Blake Nevius, *Edith Wharton: A Study of Her Fiction* (Berkeley: University of California Press, 1953).

19. Arthur Mizener, "The Age of Innocence," *Twelve Great American Novels* (New York: New American Library, 1967), 68–86.

Chapter 4

1. Wharton, "Life and I," in *Edith Wharton, Novellas and Other Writings*, 1071; hereafter cited in text as *LI*.

2. Wharton, *A Backward Glance*, in *Edith Wharton, Novellas and Other Writings*, 824; hereafter cited in text as *ABG*.

3. Edith Wharton, *The Age of Innocence* (New York: Macmillan, 1993), 5–6; hereafter cited in text.

4. Louis Auchincloss, *Edith Wharton; A Woman in Her Time* (New York: Viking, 1971), 129, 128.

5. Mary Cadwalader Jones to Edith Wharton, 22 November 1922, Yale American Literature Collection (YALC), as quoted in S. Benstock, *No Gifts from Chance*, 359.

6. Rutger B. Jewett to Edith Wharton, 13 November 1920, YALC, as quoted in Benstock, *No Gifts From Chance*, 359.

7. Edith Wharton to Mary Cadwalader Jones, 17 February 1921, in *Letters*, 439.

8. The importance of moral belief to Wharton had been ignored in much of the criticism, but in 1994 and 1995 two books that insist on her philosophical and cultural awareness have rectified this previous critical blindness. Dale Bauer and Carol J. Singley each assess Wharton as an intellectual, philosophical force.

9. Edith Wharton to Rutger B. Jewett, 5 January 1920, in *Letters*, 428.

10. Edith Wharton to Bernard Berenson, 12 December 1920, in *Letters*, 433.

11. See Shari Benstock, *No Gifts From Chance*, 49–55.

12. See Wharton's letters to Morton Fullerton from 1908 through 1911 in *Letters*, 121–215.

13. Alan Price, "The Composition of Edith Wharton's *The Age of Innocence*," *Yale University Library Gazette* 55 (July 1980), 22–30; hereafter cited in text.

Chapter 5

1.   James W. Tuttleton, *The Novel of Manners in America* (Chapel Hill: University of North Carolina Press, 1972), xi–14, 128–33; hereafter cited in text.

Chapter 6

1.   Donna M. Campbell, "Edith Wharton and the 'Authoresses': The Critique of Local Color in Wharton's Early Fiction," *Studies in American Fiction* 22, no. 2 (Autumn 1994), 169–83.

2.   Judith Fryer, *Felicitous Space: The Imaginative Structures of Edith Wharton and Willa Cather* (Chapel Hill: University of North Carolina Press, 1986), 95–115.

3.   Based on the B. Q. Morgan translation, Johann Wolfgang von Goethe, *Faust I* (New York: Appleton-Century-Crofts, 1946).

4.   Louis Auchincloss, *Edith Wharton*, 129.

5.   Arthur Mizener, *Twelve Great American Novels* (New York: New American Library, 1967), 85–86.

Chapter 7

1.   See Joseph Candido, "Edith Wharton's Final Alterations of *The Age of Innocence*," *Studies in American Fiction* 6–7 (1978–79), 21–31.

2.   Edith Wharton, *The Writing of Fiction* (New York: Scribner's, 1925), 6; hereafter cited in text as *Writing*.

Chapter 8

1.   Edith Wharton to William Gerhardi, 22 January 1931, from the Harry Ransom Humanities Research Center, University of Texas, Austin; used with permission of the collection.

2.   Grace Kellogg, *The Two Lives of Edith Wharton, The Woman and Her Work* (New York: Appleton-Century, 1965), 228.

3.   Cynthia Griffin Wolff, *A Feast of Words: The Triumph of Edith Wharton* (New York: Addison-Wesley, 1995 reissue), 306.

4.   Ibid.

5.   Ibid., 307.

6.   Ibid., 316.

Chapter 9

1.   Edith Wharton, *The Writing of Fiction*, 135; hereafter cited in text.

Notes and References

Chapter 10

1. Evelyn E. Bracasso, "The Transparent Eye of May Welland in Wharton's *The Age of Innocence*," *Modern Language Studies* 21, no. 4 (Fall 1991), 48.

Chapter 12

1. Shari Benstock, *No Gifts From Chance: A Biography of Edith Wharton* (New York: Scribner's, 1994), 362.

2. Edith Wharton, "New Year's Day," *Edith Wharton, Novellas and Other Writings*, 491.

Chapter 13

1. Quoted in Alan Price, "The Composition of Edith Wharton's *The Age of Innocence*," *Yale University Library Gazette*, 1980, 26; hereafter cited in text.

2. Shari Benstock, *Women of the Left Bank: Paris, 1900–1940* (Austin: University of Texas Press, 1986), 39–40.

3. Grace Kellogg, *The Two Lives of Edith Wharton*, 227.

4. Mary Ellis Gibson, "Edith Wharton and the Ethnography of Old New York," *Studies in American Fiction*, 1985, 67.

5. Cynthia Griffin Wolff, *A Feast of Words*, 304.

6. Ibid., 325–26.

7. Wendy Gimbel, *Edith Wharton: Orphancy and Survival* (New York: Praeger, 1984), 127.

8. See Henry James to William James in *The Correspondence of William James, vol. 2* (Charlottesville: University of Virginia Press, 1993), 394–95, 405; and see Wharton's chapter on James in *A Backward Glance*, 909–32 in *Edith Wharton, Novellas and Other Writings*.

9. Edith Wharton, "The Old Maid," in *Edith Wharton, Novellas and Other Writings*, 377; hereafter cited in text.

Bibliography

Primary Sources

Novels and Novellas

The Touchstone. New York: Scribner's, 1900.

The Valley of Decision. 2 vols. New York: Scribner's, 1902.

Sanctuary. New York: Scribner's, 1903.

The House of Mirth. New York: Scribner's, 1905.

The Fruit of the Tree. New York: Scribner's, 1907.

Madame de Treymes. New York: Scribner's, 1907.

Ethan Frome. New York: Scribner's, 1911.

The Reef. New York: Appleton, 1912.

The Custom of the Country. New York: Scribner's, 1913.

"Bunner Sisters" in *Xingu and Other Stories.* New York: Scribner's, 1916.

Summer. New York: Appleton, 1917.

The Marne. New York: Appleton, 1918.

The Age of Innocence. New York: Appleton, 1920.

The Glimpses of the Moon. New York: Appleton, 1922.

A Son at the Front. New York: Scribner's, 1923.

Old New York: False Dawn, The Old Maid, The Spark, New Year's Day. New York: Appleton, 1924.

The Mother's Recompense. New York: Appleton, 1925.

Twilight Sleep. New York: Appleton, 1927.

The Children. New York: Appleton, 1928.

Hudson River Bracketed. New York: Appleton, 1929.

Bibliography

The Gods Arrive. New York: Appleton, 1932.

The Buccaneers. New York: Appleton-Century, 1938.

Fast and Loose, a Novelette by David Olivieri, ed. Viola Hopkins Winner. Charlottesville: University Press of Virginia, 1977. Wharton's first novel, written when she was 14.

Edith Wharton, Novellas and Other Writings, ed. Cynthia Griffin Wolff. New York: Library of America, 1990.

Fast and Loose & The Buccaneers, ed. Viola Hopkins Winner. Charlottesville: University Press of Virginia, 1993.

The Buccaneers: A Novel by Edith Wharton, completed by Marion Mainwaring. New York: Viking Penguin, 1993.

Short Story Collections

The Greater Inclination. New York: Scribner's, 1899.

Crucial Instances. New York: Scribner's, 1901.

The Descent of Man and Other Stories. New York: Scribner's, 1904.

The Hermit and the Wild Woman and Other Stories. New York: Scribner's, 1908.

Tales of Men and Ghosts. New York: Scribner's, 1910.

Xingo and Other Stories. New York: Scribner's, 1916.

Here and Beyond. New York: Appleton, 1926.

Certain People. New York: Appleton, 1930.

Human Nature. New York: Appleton, 1933.

The World Over. New York: Appleton-Century, 1936.

Ghosts. New York: Appleton-Century, 1937.

The Collected Short Stories of Edith Wharton, 2 vols., ed. R. W. B. Lewis. New York: Scribner's, 1968.

The Selected Short Stories of Edith Wharton, ed. R. W. B. Lewis. New York: Scribner's, 1991.

Poetry

Verses. Newport, R.I.: C. E. Hammett, 1878.

Artemis to Actaeon and Other Verse. New York: Scribner's, 1909.

Twelve Poems. London: The Medici Society, 1926.

Travel Writing, Memoir, Criticism, Autobiography

The Decoration of Houses (with Ogden Codman, Jr.). New York: Scribner's, 1897.

Italian Villas and Their Gardens. New York: Century, 1904.

Italian Backgrounds. New York: Scribner's, 1905.

A Motor-Flight through France. New York: Scribner's, 1908.

Fighting France, from Dunkerque to Belfort. New York: Scribner's, 1915.

The Book of the Homeless (editor). New York: Scribner's, 1916.

French Ways and Their Meaning. New York: Appleton, 1919.

In Morocco. New York: Scribner's, 1920.

The Writing of Fiction. New York: Scribner's, 1925.

A Backward Glance. New York: Appleton-Century, 1934.

Translation
The Joy of Living, by Hermann Sudermann. New York: Scribner's, 1902.

Letters
The Letters of Edith Wharton, eds. R. W. B. Lewis and Nancy Lewis. New York: Scribner's, 1988.

Henry James and Edith Wharton, Letters: 1900–1915, ed. Lyall H. Powers. New York: Scribner's, 1990.

Secondary Sources

Books

Ammons, Elizabeth. *Conflicting Stories: American Women Writers at the Turn into the Twentieth Century.* New York: Oxford University Press, 1992. Examines Wharton's fiction in the context of multiracial and multiethnic women's writing during the progressive and early modernist eras.

———. *Edith Wharton's Argument with America.* Athens: University of Georgia Press, 1980. Reads the major fiction with close attention to the fact that Wharton was a woman writer, a reversal of the usual interpretations at this time.

Auchincloss, Louis. *Edith Wharton; A Woman in Her Time.* New York: Viking, 1971. Sympathetic and acute readings of Wharton's characters, with biographical and cultural information.

Bauer, Dale M. *Edith Wharton's Brave New Politics.* Madison: University of Wisconsin Press, 1994. Discusses Wharton's major fiction, particularly the later books, in relation to the history—political, medical, and sociological—of the 1920s and the 1930s.

———. *Female Dialogics: A Theory of Failed Community.* Albany: State

Bibliography

University of New York Press, 1988. Relates Wharton's work to that of Henry James, Kate Chopin, and Nathanial Hawthorne, using a Bakhtinian perspective.

Bell, Millicent. *Edith Wharton and Henry James: The Story of Their Friendship.* New York: George Braziller, 1965. Based largely on the two writers' correspondence, Bell traces the personal and writerly relationship.

Bendixen, Alfred and Annette Zilversmit, eds. *Edith Wharton: New Critical Essays.* New York: Garland, 1992. Good collection of essays, many previously unpublished.

Benstock, Shari. *No Gifts From Chance: A Biography of Edith Wharton.* New York: Scribner's, 1994. The best biography to date, using a number of new letters and manuscripts. Most importantly, viewing Wharton's writing and life from the perspective of the woman as writer.

———. *Women of the Left Bank: Paris, 1900–1940.* Austin: University of Texas Press, 1986. Places Wharton among a number of American women writers who emigrated to France.

Donovan, Josephine. *After the Fall: The Demeter-Persephone Myth in Wharton, Cather, and Glasgow.* University Park: Pennsylvania State University Press, 1989. Mythic readings of most of the important fictions.

Dwight, Eleanor. *Edith Wharton: An Extraordinary Life.* New York: Henry A. Abrams, 1994. Replete with photographs, this biography brings together a number of sources; not as definitive as Benstock.

Erlich, Gloria C. *The Sexual Education of Edith Wharton.* Berkeley: University of California Press, 1992. A psychoanalytic reading of not only the fiction but the life, with much attention to Wharton's relationship with her parents.

Fedorko, Kathy A. *Gender and the Gothic in the Fiction of Edith Wharton.* Tuscaloosa: University of Alabama Press, 1995. Through close readings of a number of short stories as well as novels, Fedorko shows the pervasive reliance on strategies of the gothic in Wharton's fiction, strategies that are inherently gendered.

Fracasso, Evelyn E. *Edith Wharton's Prisoners of Consciousness.* New York: Greenwood Press, 1994. Studies the theme of imprisonment throughout Wharton's stories; extensions can be made to her longer fiction.

Fryer, Judith. *Felicitous Space: The Imaginative Structures of Edith Wharton and Willa Cather.* Chapel Hill: University of North Carolina Press, 1986. Approaches the work of each writer from the perspective of the "interconnectedness between space and the female imagination."

Gilbert, Sandra M. and Susan Gubar. *No Man's Land,* vol. 2, *Sexchanges.* New Haven, Conn: Yale University Press, 1989. Treats Wharton's writing in the context of other Progressive Era writers, among them Henry James, with attention to her revisioning of form and traditional writing practices.

Gimbel, Wendy. *Edith Wharton: Orphancy and Survival.* New York: Praeger, 1984. A quasi-biographical reading of the major texts, with emphasis on the symbolic use of home/house and the importance of family.

Goodman, Susan. *Edith Wharton's Inner Circle.* Austin: University of Texas Press, 1994. Biographical study of the (mostly male) group of friends that interacted with Wharton, and helped her develop aesthetic underlying principles in her fiction.

———. *Edith Wharton's Women: Friends and Rivals.* Hanover, N.H.: University Press of New England, 1990. Discusses Wharton's friendships with key women (among them, Sara Norton), and her use of the marriage plot. Comparisons with Cather, Austin, and Glasgow.

Hadley, Kathy Miller. *In the Interstices of the Tale: Edith Wharton's Narrative Strategies.* New York: Peter Lang, 1993. Important reading of the major Wharton novels from the perspective of quasi-modernist technique and beliefs about character interaction.

Holbrook, David. *Edith Wharton and the Unsatisfactory Man.* New York: St. Martin's, 1991. Psychobiographical study of what Holbrook sees as Wharton's constant dissatisfaction with male characters.

Howe, Irving, ed. *Edith Wharton, A Collection of Critical Essays.* Englewood Cliffs, N. J.: Prentice-Hall, 1962. Retrospective collection of essays, from the 1920s to the present.

Joslin, Katherine. *Edith Wharton.* New York: St. Martin's, 1991. Very good introductory study of Wharton and her major fictions. Concise, thorough, sometimes witty.

——— and Alan Price, eds. *"Wretched Exotic": Essays on Edith Wharton in Europe.* New York: Peter Lang, 1993. Essays by various critics, most of them presented at the Wharton in Paris conference, 1991.

Kaplan, Amy. *The Social Construction of American Realism.* Chicago: University of Chicago Press, 1988. Good readings of Wharton's earlier fictions, with particular attention to economic and cultural tropes.

Kellogg, Grace. *The Two Lives of Edith Wharton, The Woman and Her Work.* New York: Appleton-Century, 1965. Sensible readings of both the life and the work; emphasis on Wharton as woman author was new for the time.

Lawson, Richard H. *Edith Wharton.* New York: Ungar, 1976. Good introductory study, with a psychoanalytic emphasis.

Lewis. R. W. B. *Edith Wharton: A Biography.* New York: Harper & Row, 1975. The prizewinning first biography that helped establish Wharton as an author to be studied anew.

Lindberg, Gary H. *Edith Wharton and the Novel of Manners.* Charlottesville: University Press of Virginia, 1975. Discussion of the fiction as social commentary.

Bibliography

Lubbock, Percy. *Portrait of Edith Wharton*. New York: Appleton-Century-Crofts, 1947. Informal memoir, with no attempt to be scholarly or comprehensive.

McDowell, Margaret. *Edith Wharton*. Boston: Twayne, 1976; revised, 1990. While the first book was important, accurate, and thorough, the second (much more than a revision) is truly fine.

Nevius, Blake. *Edith Wharton: A Study of Her Fiction*. Berkeley: University of California Press, 1953. First major study of the fiction, with attention to Wharton's theme of individual fulfillment versus community.

Rae, Catherine M. *Edith Wharton's New York Quartet*. Lanham, Md.: University Press of America, 1984. Close readings of the four novellas, with contextualizing information.

Raphael, Lev. *Edith Wharton's Prisoners of Shame*. New York: St. Martin's, 1991. Thematic study of the way Wharton's early experiences influenced her views of women's character.

Singley, Carol J. *Edith Wharton: Matters of Mind and Spirit*. New York: Cambridge University Press, 1995. The first study to place Wharton's work within mainstream philosophic and religious currents. Brings a new definition to Wharton's intellectualism.

Tuttleton, James. *The Novel of Manners in America*. Chapel Hill: University of North Carolina Press, 1972. Defines the type to include a number of works by Wharton.

Wagner-Martin, Linda. *The House of Mirth: A Novel of Admonition*. Boston: Twayne, 1990. Discusses Wharton's choices in all aspects of Lily Bart's story, particularly friendships and suitors; attention to narrative structures, scenic organization, and metaphor.

Waid, Candace. *Edith Wharton's Letters from the Underworld*. Chapel Hill: University of North Carolina Press, 1991. With extensive use of new materials, this thematic study provides good insight into many novels and stories.

Wershoven, Carol. *The Female Intruder in the Novels of Edith Wharton*. Rutherford, N.J.: Fairleigh Dickinson University Press, 1982. Sets up patterns for Wharton's use of strong women characters, and defines the "intruder" as an outsider critical of social norms who yet brings positive values to the culture.

White, Barbara A. *Edith Wharton: A Study of the Short Fiction*. Boston: Twayne, 1991. Insightful readings of the short fiction, with particular focus on themes of sexual abuse and incest.

Wolff, Cynthia Griffin. *A Feast of Words: The Triumph of Edith Wharton*. New York: Oxford University Press, 1977; reissued (expanded) by Addison Wesley (New York, 1995). Psychoanalytic study of the work and the life; still a premier work in the field.

————, ed. *Edith Wharton, Novellas and Other Writings* (including "Life and I"). New York: Library of America, 1990.

Essays

Ballorain, Rollande. "From Childhood to Womanhood (or from Fusion to Fragmentation): a study of the Growing up Process in 20th Century American Women's Fiction," *Revue Francaise d'Etudes Americaines* 6, no. 2 (1981), 97–112.

Blackall, Jean Frantz. "Edith Wharton's Art of Ellipsis," *Journal of Narrative Technique* 17 (1987), 145–61.

————. "The Intrusive Voice: Telegrams in *The House of Mirth* and *The Age of Innocence*," *Women's Studies* 20, no. 2 (1991), 163–68.

Bracasso, Evelyn E. "The Transparent Eyes of May Welland in Wharton's *The Age of Innocence*," *Modern Language Studies* 21 (Fall 1991), 43–48.

Candido, Joseph. "Edith Wharton's Final Alterations of *The Age of Innocence*," *Studies in American Fiction* 6–7 (1978–79), 21–31.

Colquitt, Clare. "Unpacking Her Treasures: Edith Wharton's 'Mysterious Correspondence' with Morton Fullerton." *Library Chronicle of the University of Texas* 2, no. 31 (1985), 73–107.

Cuddy, Lois A. "Triangles of Defeat and Liberation: The Quest for Power in Edith Wharton's Fiction," *Perspectives on Contemporary Literature* 8 (1982), 18–26.

Davis, Linette. "Vulgarity and Red Blood in *The Age of Innocence*," *Journal of the Midwest Modern Language Association* 20 (Fall 1987), 1–8.

Dekker, George. *The American Historical Romance.* Cambridge: Cambridge University Press, 1987, 265–71.

Eby, Clare Virginia. "Silencing Women in Edith Wharton's *The Age of Innocence*," *Colby Library Quarterly* 28 (1992), 93–104.

Evans, Elizabeth. "Musical Allusions in *The Age of Innocence*," *Notes on Contemporary Literature* 4 (1974), 4–7.

Gargano, James W. "Tableaux of Renunciation: Wharton's Use of *The Shaughran* in *The Age of Innocence*," *Studies in American Fiction* 15 (Spring 1987), 1–11.

Gibson, Mary Ellis. "Edith Wharton and the Ethnography of Old New York," *Studies in American Fiction* 13 (Spring 1985), 57–69.

Gribben, Alan. "'The Heart Is Insatiable': A Selection from Edith Wharton's Letters to Morton Fullerton, 1907–1915," *Library Chronicle of the University of Texas* 2, no. 31 (1985), 7–18.

Miller, D. Quentin. "'A Barrier of Words': The Tension Between Narrative Voice and Vision in the Writings of Edith Wharton," *American Literary Realism* 27, no. 2 (Fall 1994), 11–22.

Bibliography

Mizener, Arthur. *Twelve Great American Novels*. New York: New American Library, 1967.

Morgan, Gwendolyn. "The Unsung Heroine—A Study of May Welland in *The Age of Innocence*," *Heroines of Popular Culture*, ed. Pat Browne. Bowling Green, Ohio: Bowling Green University Popular Press, 1987, 32–40.

Nathan, Rhoda. "Ward McAllister: Beau Nash of *The Age of Innocence*," *College Literature* 14 (Fall 1987), 277–84.

O'Neal, Michael J. "Point of View and Narrative Technique in the Fiction of Edith Wharton," *Style* 17 (1983), 270–79.

Price, Alan. "The Composition of Edith Wharton's *The Age of Innocence*," *Yale University Library Gazette* 55 (July 1980), 22–30.

Richards, Mary Margaret. "'Feminized Men' in Wharton's *Old New York*," *Edith Wharton Newsletter* 3 (Fall 1986), 2–3, 12.

Robinson, James A. "Psychological Determinism in *The Age of Innocence*," *Markham Review* 5 (1975), 1–5.

Saunders, Judith P. "Becoming the Mask: Edith Wharton's Ingenues," *Massachusetts Studies in English* 7, no. 4 (1982), 33–39.

Sensibar, Judith. "Edith Wharton Reads the Bachelor Type: Her Critique of Modernism's Representative Man," *American Literature* 60, no. 4 (December 1988), 575–90.

Strout, Cushing. "Complementary Portraits: James' *Lady* and Wharton's *Age*," *Hudson Review* 35 (1982), 405–15.

Tintner, Adeline R. "Jamesean Structures in *The Age of Innocence* and Related Stories," *Twentieth Century Literature* 26 (1980), 332–47.

———. "The Narrative Structure of *Old New York*: Text and Pictures in Edith Wharton's Quartet of Linked Short Stories," *Journal of Narrative Technique* 17 (Winter 1987), 76–82.

Vidal, Gore. "Of Writers and Class: In Praise of Edith Wharton," *Atlantic* 241 (February 1978), 64–67.

Wegener, Frederick. "Edith Wharton and the Difficult Writing of *The Writing of Fiction*," *Modern Language Studies* 25, no. 2 (Spring 1995), 60–79.

White, Barbara A. "Neglected Areas: Wharton's Short Stories and Incest," *Edith Wharton Review* 8, no. 1 (Spring 1991), 3–12 and 8 no. 2 (Fall 1991), 3–10, 32.

Widmer, Eleanor. "Edith Wharton: The Nostalgia for Innocence," *The Twenties: Fiction, Poetry, Drama*, ed. Warren French. Deland, Florida: Everett/Edwarrds, Inc., 1975, 27–38.

Wilson, Edmund. "Justice to Edith Wharton," *The Wound and the Bow*, New York: Oxford University Press, 1947, 195–213.

Bibliographies

Bendixen, Alfred. "A Guide to Wharton Criticism, 1976–1983," *Edith Wharton Newsletter* 2 (1985): 1–8. Comments by others included.

———. "New Directions in Wharton Criticism: A Bibliographic Essay," *Edith Wharton Review* 10, no. 2 (Fall 1993), 20–24.

———. "Recent Wharton Studies: A Bibliographic Essay," *Edith Wharton Newsletter* 3 (1986): 5, 8–9.

———. "Wharton Studies, 1986–1987: A Bibliographic Essay," *Edith Wharton Newsletter* 5 (1988): 5–8, 10.

———. "The World of Wharton Criticism: A Bibliographic Essay," *Edith Wharton Review* 7, no. 1 (Spring 1990), 18–21.

Brenni, Vito J. *Edith Wharton: A Bibliography*. Morgantown, Va.: McClain Printing Co., 1966.

Garrison, Stephen, ed. *Edith Wharton: A Descriptive Bibliography*. Pittsburgh: University of Pittsburgh Press, 1990.

Joslin, Katherine. "Edith Wharton at 125," *College Literature* 14, no. 3 (1987), 193–206.

Lauer, Kristin O. and Margaret P. Murray, eds. *Edith Wharton: An Annotated Secondary Bibliography*. New York: Garland Publishing, 1990.

Schriber, Mary Suzanne. "Edith Wharton and the French Critics, 1906–1937," *American Literary Realism* 13 (1980), 61–72.

Springer, Marlene, ed. *Edith Wharton and Kate Chopin: A Reference Guide*. Boston: G. K. Hall, 1976.

——— and Joan Gilson, eds. "Edith Wharton: A Reference Guide Updated," *Resources in American Literary Study* 14 (Spring and Autumn 1984), 85–111.

Tuttleton, James W. "Edith Wharton" in *American Women Writers: Bibliographical Essays*, eds. Maurice Duke, Jackson R. Bryer, and M. Thomas Inge. Westport, Conn.: Greenwood Press, 1983, 71–107. Updates his original essay in *Resources for American Literary Study* 3 (1973).

———, Kristin O. Lauer, and Margaret P. Murray, eds. *Edith Wharton: The Contemporary Reviews*. New York: Cambridge University Press, 1992.

Zilversmit, Annette. "Appendix, Bibliographical Index," *College Literature* 14 (1987), 305–9.

Index

Index

The Author

Linda Wagner-Martin is Hanes Professor of English and Comparative Literature at the University of North Carolina, Chapel Hill. Recent books are *"Favored Strangers": Gertrude Stein and Her Family*; *Telling Women's Lives, The New Biography*; and *The Modern American Novel, 1914–1945*. She is coeditor of *The Oxford Companion to Women's Writing* in the United States and its accompanying anthology of women's writing, and of *New Essays on William Faulkner's* Go Down, Moses. Her other books in this series are on Edith Wharton's The *House of Mirth* and Sylvia Plath's *The Bell Jar*. In addition to having served as president of the Ernest Hemingway Foundation and Society for the past three years, she is a past president of the Society for the Study of Narrative and incoming president of the American Literature division of the MLA.